CELEBRATING

50

SONGS *of* PRAISE

YEARS

TREVOR BARNES

Foreword by Aled Jones

LION

Copyright © 2011 Trevor Barnes
This edition copyright © 2011 Lion Hudson
The author asserts the moral right
to be identified as the author of this work

A Lion Book
an imprint of
Lion Hudson plc
Wilkinson House, Jordan Hill Road,
Oxford OX2 8DR, England
www.lionhudson.com
ISBN 978 0 7459 5384 7
Distributed by:

UK: Marston Book Services, PO Box 269,
Abingdon, Oxon OX14 4YN
USA: Trafalgar Square Publishing,
814 N. Franklin Street, Chicago, IL 60610
USA Christian Market: Kregel Publications,
PO Box 2607, Grand Rapids, MI 49501

First edition 2011
10 9 8 7 6 5 4 3 2 1 0
All rights reserved

A catalogue record for this book is available
from the British Library

Typeset in Bell MT 10/12 and
Humanist 777 BT 11/12

Printed and bound in China

CELEBRATING

5 SONGS of PRAISE

YEARS

Contents

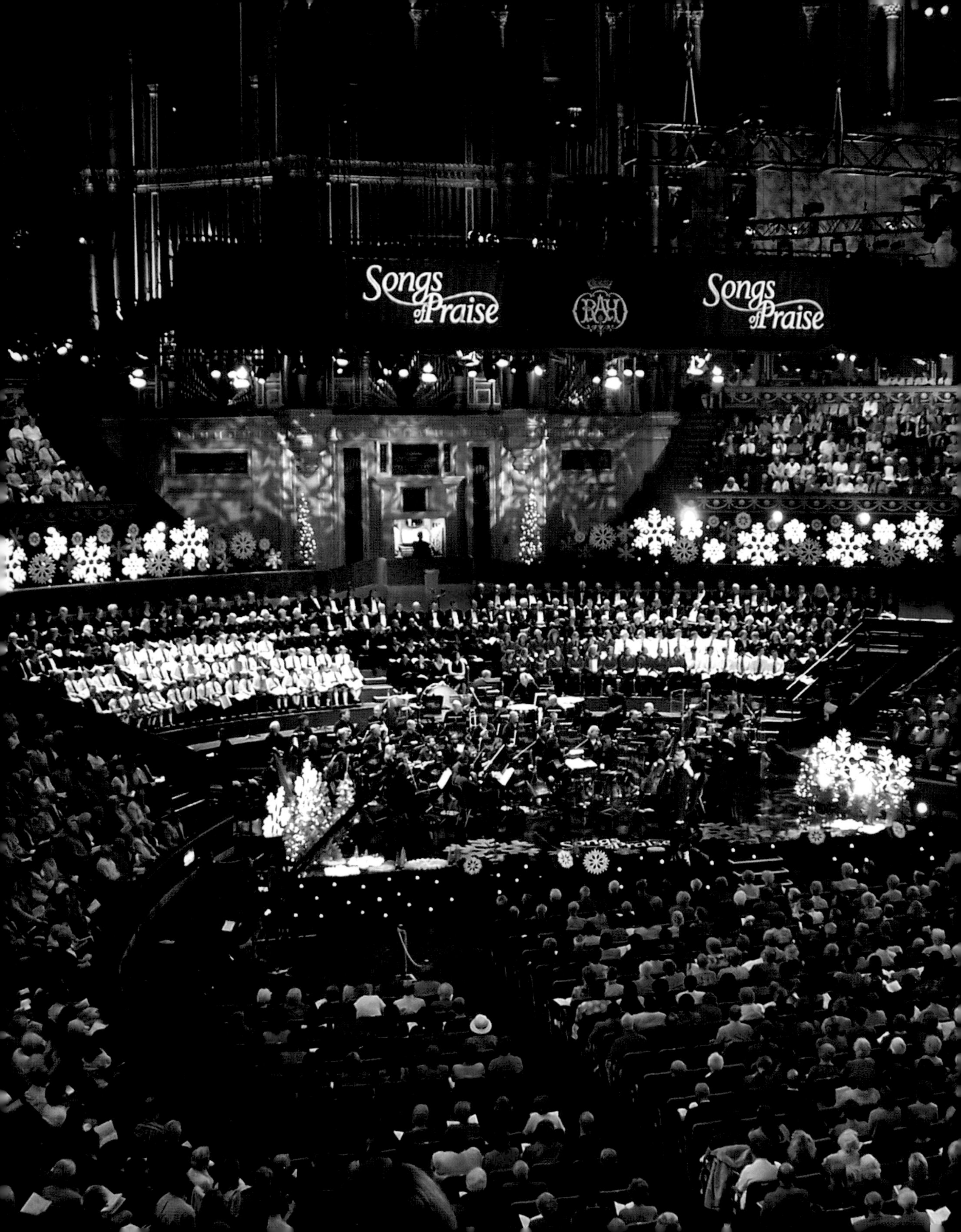

Foreword
by Aled Jones

Not only is *Songs of Praise* marking its fiftieth anniversary but I can't believe that it is eleven years since I was first invited to present the programme! It has been an amazing decade and a wonderful opportunity to meet so many people, visit so many places, and sing so many hymns!

I have travelled the length and breadth of the United Kingdom, filming for the programme in such a variety of situations. And I've also had the chance to experience *Songs of Praise* overseas – from Spain to South Africa, from Israel to the Falkland Islands.

I've also always enjoyed returning to the land of my birth and singing my heart out with some of our great hymns. There's nothing to blow the cobwebs away like a rousing rendition of "Cwm Rhondda"!

As Trevor Barnes reminds us in this comprehensive account, it all began in Wales. That first broadcast from the Tabernacle Baptist Chapel in Cardiff gave birth to a remarkable television tradition. And here we are, fifty years later, continuing to provide inspirational singing, captivating stories of faith, and a moment to pause in the hurly burly of life.

Many things have changed in that time – but many things have also remained the same. And it is the faith of people, the timeless music, and the surprising places that still make up the successful mix that we call *Songs of Praise* today.

I know you will be fascinated to read the story so far. You will get a glimpse behind the scenes into how the programmes are so carefully made. You will meet some of those responsible for the shape of the series. And you will hear what's in store for the future.

Whether you're a season ticket holder or a newcomer to *Songs of Praise*, this will be a book you will want to read more than once.

All the best – and thanks for watching!

Aled Jones

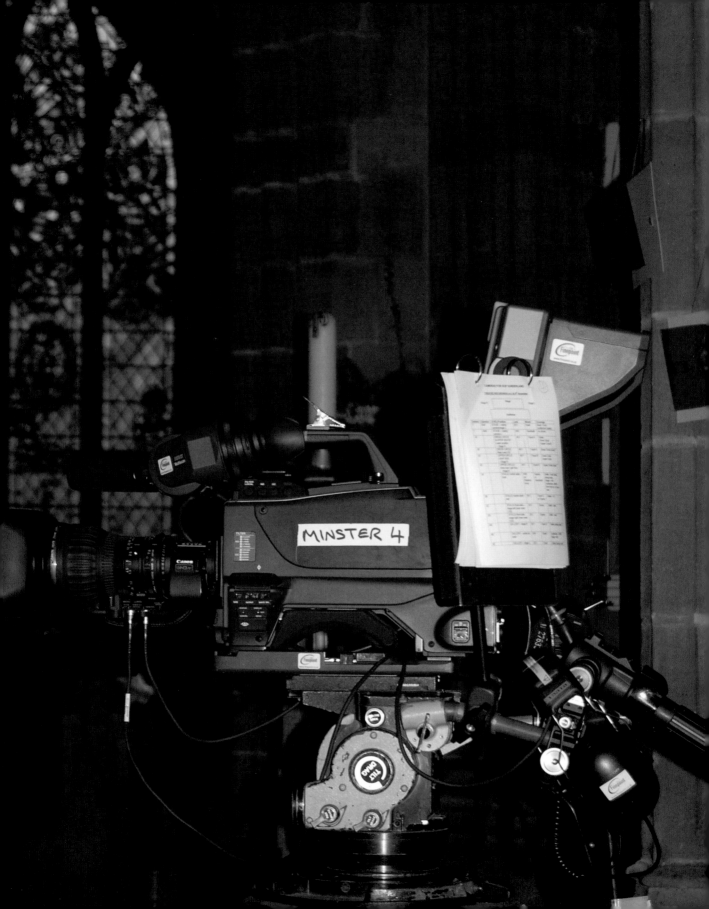

Preface by Tommy Nagra

I am in an incredibly privileged position – to oversee one of Britain's most iconic and flagship television programmes is a great honour and one that brings great responsibility.

As custodian of one of the BBC's biggest brands, our Jubilee year is a great time to mark and celebrate the joy of *Songs of Praise* and its place in the hearts and minds of the great British public. It is, after all, the only show of its kind, and the longest running religious TV programme in the world. Millions of viewers tune in every week and since the very first programme in 1961, it has gone on to cement its place as an essential part of the Sunday TV experience.

In a fast-changing and ever-evolving broadcasting landscape, *Songs of Praise* has remained a steadfast and familiar destination for our viewers. I remember growing up in the 1970s and hearing the theme tune, which for me signalled the end of the weekend… and school the following morning!

As you will see in this commemorative book, the programme has evolved over fifty years. While the people, body, and packaging may have changed, the heart remains very much rooted in a musical celebration of the Christian faith. Just like the very first programmes, congregational singing remains the bedrock of the show and we take great pride in ensuring the standards of production are of the highest possible quality.

Since taking over the reins of the programme, I have been amazed by the deep connection the programme has with its loyal audience. The emails that come in on a Monday are full of viewers' comments – often praising the programme from the day before… and sometimes telling us when we've got it wrong. What is undeniable is that the overwhelming feedback – good and bad – is written with great affection for our programme and we take great care to respond to each and every letter and email.

This bond with our audience is crucial to the continued success of *Songs of Praise*; the people in our audience are the essential ingredient and real stars of the programme's format – without congregations coming along to sing, we haven't got a show! The recording of hymns and music in churches and other venues across the country is a joyous experience where we get to meet our audience face to face; it's a priceless insight into why, after fifty years, the show remains as strong as ever.

Our anniversary year is an opportunity to celebrate the people and stories that have made *Songs of Praise* the institution that it is. But anniversaries are not just for looking backwards. They are for looking forward too, and I can assure you my team based in Manchester are striving hard to deliver the next phase of its evolution, ensuring that tomorrow's programmes are every bit as popular as those of yesterday.

Photographs from the programme's archive take us back in time to a very different social and broadcasting landscape from that of today. But what looks quaintly dated and old fashioned to our technologically sophisticated eyes was once brand new and cutting edge. The challenge for us is to embrace the new digital age and take the programme forward while still keeping faith with its original vision. As patterns of Christian worship change, so too does the programme. Year by year, week by week, we aspire to bring you inspirational music and stories of ordinary people doing extraordinary things.

This book is a tribute to the staff, past and present, all of whom have been committed to delivering the highest standards of production week in, week out, for half a century. As we have all discovered, once you've worked on *Songs of Praise*, it never leaves you.

Happy reading.

Tommy Nagra,
BBC's Head of Television,
Religion and Ethics

A diverse range of outside broadcast trucks in use in the 1960s, including on the right, the latest Bedord TK – the quintessential light truck in the UK through most of the sixties and seventies.

Introduction

One down. Only 2,500 more to go

Historic moments are easily missed. Who in the autumn of 1961, for instance, could have watched the Revd Dr Gwilym ap Robert, minister turned TV presenter, standing before a slightly bewildered congregation at the Tabernacle Baptist Chapel in Cardiff and realised that a broadcasting tradition was being forged before their eyes? Who would have guessed that they were witnessing the birth of a phenomenon that would endure for half a century, change the nation's Sunday evening viewing habits for ever, and establish itself as one of the longest running television programmes of all time?

Not, probably, Gethyn Stoodley Thomas, the producer of that first programme who, like countless other producers and directors after him, was running on pure adrenalin and merely hoping that the knobs he was twiddling in the outside broadcast (OB) unit backstage were actually connected to something front of house. Poised between triumph and disgrace he would have had to defer his appreciation

of that historic moment for another forty minutes or so until the programme had been recorded. Only then would a relieved, elated, and much older man emerge from the control booth to take the credit for his part in the inaugural edition of *Songs of Praise*. One down. Only 2,500 more to go.

"Faith matters – and Songs of Praise *echoes that in song and story."*

David Taviner, series editor

Three decades later

Three decades later, in the spring of 1993, director Chris Mann is occupying the Stoodley Thomas memorial hot seat. In the course of the afternoon Chris will record congregational hymn-singing just as his distinguished predecessor had done in Cardiff, but there the similarities between the two events diverge dramatically.

First, the Baptist chapel has been replaced by a hangar at RAF Scampton in Lincolnshire, bedecked with flowers to celebrate the fiftieth anniversary of 617 Squadron's attack on the dams of

the Ruhr; secondly, the number of knobs, levers, buttons, and switches on the BBC control panel has increased beyond all recognition; and thirdly, the Red Arrows aerobatic display team is closing in on proceedings

The Red Arrows in formation.

Inset: Rehearsal at RAF Scampton in 1993.

*"People could
say that here was
another telly person
playing around
with expensive
toys. But no. My
vision was deeply
evangelistic."*

**Chris Mann,
former producer**

he fades up camera 1 and tracks
the planes' approach right to left.
Seconds later he cuts to camera
2, shoots them doubling back in
tight formation to the right of the
screen and establishes contact with
the lead pilot 1,000 feet above him,
and cues the smoke. Red, white,
and blue vapour trails emerge
from the aircraft in perfect time to
the music and cross-fade tastefully
into the Central Band of the RAF,
and we are once again earthbound
in expectation of another evening
of song. Meanwhile several
million *Songs of Praise* viewers are
rearranging their bottoms on sofas
up and down the land or balancing
cups of tea on their knees, unaware
of all the excitement that is
happening just off the A15.

at a speed of around 450 mph,
expecting to be choreographed
into shot at precisely the moment
the band strikes up with the
opening bars of the Dambusters
March. Even Chris, unflappable
and in control at the tensest of live

broadcasting moments, is outside
his comfort zone.

He has instructed the BBC
television continuity announcer to
come to him at transmission time
"plus or minus no seconds", and he
waits for his cue. When it comes

Below: The *School Choir of The Year* judges (l–r): David Grant, Claire Sweeney, and Howard Goodall.

Below right: Finalists of Songs of Praise: Senior School Choir of The Year (l–r): St Aidan's Church of England High School, Harrogate, North Yorkshire; Maria Fidelis Convent School, London (the eventual winners); and Rugby High School.

Spring of 2010

Advance the calendar to the spring of 2010 and a BBC OB crew is working through the night rigging the Queen Elizabeth Hall in London. Tons of scaffolding and lights and miles of cabling are being distributed around the auditorium in preparation for a musical event that looks as if it owes more to the *Eurovision Song Contest* or *Pop Idol* than it does to a programme of congregational hymn-singing. During the next day's recording an invited audience will be encouraged to wave their banners and mascots, cheer on their favourite choirs, and sit back to listen to the People's Tenor, Russell Watson, belting out an aria as they await the results of the School Choir of The Year.

The production has all the trappings of the slickest light entertainment shows. Lights flash, computer graphics roll, cameras rise and swoop, and throbbing background music ramps up the tension as the winners are announced. It is a total success and tremendous fun. The audience is ecstatic and goes home with a spring in its step, confident that, for this event alone, it has got every penny's worth of the annual television licence fee.

Surely these events cannot be *Songs of Praise*? Surely such rollicking extravaganzas cannot be part of the same strand that broadcast the formal, slightly staid hymn-singing from Cardiff all those years ago?

Well, actually they can. And this fiftieth anniversary book will attempt to explain why *Songs of Praise* continues to delight, entertain, and uplift – if occasionally challenging and irritating – its loyal audience of up to 3 million viewers, week in, week out, fifty-two Sundays a year, every year. Not only that, the book will try to show how the programme manages to stay true to its original intention while simultaneously

> *"I've never worked on any programme that has had the same connection with its audience."*
>
> **Tommy Nagra, executive producer**

adapting itself to the changing fashions and demands of the twenty-first century.

It is not an easy task, but it is one that the *Songs of Praise* team knows it avoids at its peril. The programme's producers and directors, editors and researchers, production managers and engineering personnel meet, week after week, trying to devise different ways of doing the same thing. The production meetings (and the accompanying appraisals of the previous week's programme) have changed in size and focus over the years, but essentially they have been happening for half a century, ensuring quality control is in the hands of the programme's fiercest critics – its staff. But the producers and directors, the researchers and technical managers do not operate in a bubble, quarantined from their audience. Every week they read hundreds of letters and emails from appreciative, delighted, demanding, and sometimes disgruntled viewers asking for this or that, praising a particular programme, complaining about another, enquiring about a hymn, and suggesting ideas. Viewers communicate with them as they would with valued and trusted members of a long-standing family business in which they have a personal stake. Every communication is read and every suggestion considered, in a process that has lasted for fifty years.

Enduring success

So what is the secret of *Songs of Praise*'s enduring success?

A hint as to the programme's longevity can be found, appropriately enough, in the second verse of one of the best-known and best-loved hymns in the English language: "Abide with Me", a favourite in the *Songs of*

> *"Songs of Praise conveys something of the human spirit."*

Liz Barr, former researcher

Praise canon. In it the hymn-writer Henry Francis Lyte examines and celebrates the omnipresence of God in the ups and downs of our earthly lives, praying finally that the grace and goodness of the divine will accompany us to the grave and beyond. "Change and decay in all around I see" are the words conventionally sung, but some scholars have argued that "change *or* decay" may have been the words originally written.

The implication is clear: earthly things either change and move on or they remain fixed and perish. Only the prime mover, Lyte may have been suggesting, is the same yesterday, today, and tomorrow. We, frail creatures of flesh and bone,

must change to survive. And what frailer creation is there (albeit not of flesh and bone) than a television programme, here today and often gone tomorrow?

Growing ambitions

So where do we look for the foundations on which success has been built? A good starting point is the transmission archive. A glance down the long list of broadcast programmes reveals a fairly consistent choice of venue in the early days – Zion English Baptist Church in Newtown, Chapel Street Methodist Church in Penzance, Mayflower Methodist Church in

Leicester – small Nonconformist venues which were doubtless well attended by local worshippers and which provided a substantial, ready-made congregation for a couple of BBC cameras to film.

Even as early as 1962, however, the team's growing ambitions were becoming clear, as they chose larger locations such as the cathedrals of Guildford and (the following year) Manchester. Pretty soon, with the programme firmly established in the schedule, producers were going for even grander settings, targeting the great medieval cathedrals of Durham, Wells, and St Albans, while also including less obviously religious locations such as the US air force base in West Ruislip

Cameramen set up a "High Seat Falcon Dolly" outside St Giles' Cathedral in Edinburgh, June 1977. Use of the Falcon enabled the camera to film interesting views from higher vantage points as it could rise to over eight feet.

Durham Cathedral stands out above the skyline.

(1969), Strangeways Prison in Manchester (1982), the Varieties Music Hall in Leeds (1994), the Chelsea Flower Show (2003), and Charles Darwin's birthplace (2009).

From the Isle of Wight to Dunoon, from Runcorn to Barnet, from Treorchy to Billericay, the *Songs of Praise* caravan has traversed the British Isles with indefatigable enthusiasm. In fifty years it has met the well-dressers of Buxton, the prisoners of Maidstone, and the holiday-makers of Torquay. It has been welcomed at Butlin's and Eton, has been at home with personalities as various as Cliff Richard, Laura Ashley, and Lord Soper and, with its international link-ups, has joined hands with singers and worshippers in Tonga and Kenya, Johannesburg, Jamaica, and Jerusalem.

From the 2009 Viewers' Questionnaire

How would you describe *Songs of Praise* in no more than ten words?

- Heart-warming, uplifting, bringing a Christian presence into every home.
- A unique British tradition praising God.
- A very special programme that brings happiness and peace to the soul.
- An oasis of Christian music and an encouragement to faith.
- A chink of traditional faith in an increasingly secular world.
- Essential, calming, uplifting, fun for young and old alike.
- A programme that shows religion at its best.
- A calm oasis in a troubled world.
- The best advertisement that Christian worship isn't dead.
- A national treasure.

17

A broadcasting milestone

In the 1990s *Songs of Praise* began to think really big and dreamt up vast spectaculars attracting tens of thousands of people to the football grounds of Old Trafford and Goodison Park. Once the team had got the taste for big events there was no stopping them, or their ambition. Their inventiveness and innovation culminated in the January 2000 edition of *Songs of Praise*, which came from the Millennium Stadium, Cardiff, attracted an unprecedented live audience of 60,000 and, with TV viewers watching in their millions,

established itself as a broadcasting milestone.

But if the programme has provided uplifting entertainment for a mass audience it has also been there on more sombre occasions to commemorate moments of national grief or tragedy.

Three live programmes marking the outbreak of the first Gulf War, for instance, generated some of the largest television audiences the programme had ever logged. *Songs of Praise* editors did not,

however, take the credit for this reaction or rush to crow about the record ratings the programme had produced. Instead they went quietly (and swiftly) about the business of responding to a national mood. The programmes were careful to avoid any sense of triumphalism, and indeed the third of them, from Dunblane Cathedral, sensitively reflected the anti-war feelings that had been widespread in Scotland and elsewhere.

Five years later, in March 1996, Dunblane Cathedral was also the setting for one of the most poignant editions the team and the audience can remember. It was broadcast just four days after a gunman had rampaged through the

L–r: Chris Mann (producer), Angela Groves (production assistant), and Geoffrey Wheeler (presenter).

local primary school, taking the lives of sixteen children and one adult before turning one of his four loaded revolvers on himself.

Crucially, and typically, the *Songs of Praise* team came to Dunblane not as intrusive outsiders searching for sensational headlines but as welcome visitors who could be trusted to handle the rawness of people's emotions with the utmost sensitivity and professionalism. Those emotions were broadcast – on Mothering Sunday of all days – in the shared hope that this would help a grieving community along the painful road toward some kind of healing.

The death of Diana, Princess of Wales, was another national event that highlighted the team's sensitivity and professionalism. They were responding to a phenomenon the like of which the country had never witnessed before. The country's entire television schedules had been remade from scratch, but a single announcement on BBC television news that a special service was to be broadcast live from St Paul's Cathedral that evening generated crowds in their thousands queueing to take part.

Left: A mourning couple comfort each other as they view floral tributes to mark the death of children in a shooting tragedy in Dunblane, Scotland, 1996.

"*Songs of Praise* was never just another programme. It was always much more than that. To me it felt more like a responsibility. There was definitely a religious purpose behind the way I approached it. It would have been perfectly possible to write some words and learn them, but unless those words really meant something to you and you meant what you said, it was never going to work. It was a marvellous programme to work on and a great privilege to meet people and hear their stories of courage and faith. People would talk to you in ways that they might not to a friend or even a member of the family and they would open themselves up to you. I think they did that because they knew we could be trusted. I also tried to put myself in the position of the viewers at home, many of whom might not be able to get to church. There is a great nostalgia for the old hymns, the ones people still remember from their childhood. I thought putting the words on-screen was a terrific way of keeping them alive and of letting everyone join in. From an insider's point of view, however, it was extremely rewarding to be working with a team of top-class professionals who cared about their work, cared about the programme, and cared about the people. It was always a huge community event and a great occasion."

> *"We are invited into people's lives and, most of all, we are trusted."*
>
> **Geoffrey Wheeler, former presenter**

Geoffrey Wheeler

Favourite hymns:
"*O, Jesus, I Have Promised*", "*Lord of All Hopefulness*".

This is what *Songs of Praise* is about: celebrating and reflecting, and at times mourning and commemorating, the lives of people throughout England, Wales, Scotland, and Northern Ireland. It is about communities and the men, women, and children who make those communities live and breathe. People are the heartbeat of the programme, and it is people who have made the programme last so long.

Consider this. A TV costume drama comes to town. The local

press has interviews with the stars,
the high street is covered with mud
and straw, shops and houses are
given a Hardy, Austen, or Dickens
makeover, and shooting goes on for
a fortnight. In that time, because of
the nature of television drama, the
crew must shoot on a closed set or,
at most, one that is cordoned off
from the public. You may glimpse
Colin Firth and Judi Dench in the
distance but it is highly unlikely that
you will be able to talk at length
to them – not because they are
standoffish or aloof but because of
the demands of the schedule and the
shoot.

Songs of Praise, by contrast,
arrives in town and
actively opens its arms
to the community. It
wants to meet the people
and wants the people to
strike up a relationship
with its researchers and
presenters. In the week
prior to the programme,
and especially in the
frenetic two-day rehearsal

Top: Filming a feature about Charles
Dickens in Kent.

Middle: Valetta Stallabrass, researcher,
sets off on one of the many journeys
made in the course of research.

Bottom: Pam Rhodes engages with an
audience while filming in Barbados.

Left: An OB unit on a ferry on its way to film *Songs of Praise* along the Clyde. Four stops with a different choir singing at each, with just one hour's set-up time at each stop!

and recording period, it is "access all areas". People are able to chat to technicians and producers, to ask questions of lighting designers and sound engineers, even to get Alan Titchmarsh, Aled Jones, and Pam Rhodes to sign a few autographs. And Pam is not alone in having made lots of lasting friendships with people who, just a few days earlier, had been strangers. An instantly recognisable face wherever she goes she delights in talking to her audience in even the most ordinary of locations. "I never mind if people come up to me in supermarkets," she says fondly, "because friends have time for friends."

On 19 November 2009 the people of Cockermouth in Cumbria braced themselves for yet another downpour. Already flooded after days of persistent rain, the town was expecting the worst and would not be disappointed. In a single day the surrounding hills were to be hit by the highest rainfall levels ever recorded in UK history, sending millions of gallons of water into the already swollen rivers Cocker and Derwent, claiming the life of a local

police officer, and destroying the homes and livelihoods of hundreds of people already caught up in the devastating floods. Television news reporters descended on the town and relayed dramatic pictures of householders being winched to safety by helicopter or ferried to dry land by lifeboat crews brought in from the coast. Government ministers travelled to the scene; the emergency services worked around the clock; and local people who had lived and worked in the town anonymously all their lives were suddenly thrust into the glare of the TV lights to provide eye-witness accounts of the devastation. The floods, of course, receded, and with them the front page headlines. And just as quickly as the cameras and microphones had appeared they vanished from view as the national news media departed to report on the next natural disaster somewhere else.

The local press, however, continued to report on the massive clean-up operation that followed, among them BBC Radio Cumbria, which now examined how local people were rebuilding a normal

Above: The emergency services swing into action in the flooded streets of Cockermouth.

Top: Director David Kremer rehearsing in the scanner.

Below: A special programme celebrating the resilience of the close-knit Cockermouth community was broadcast in February 2010.

life after the trauma of the flooding. In the process they discovered another story that had gone largely unreported: the crucial role that local churches had played in providing personnel and premises to help a community in distress. The *Songs of Praise* production team in Manchester responded quickly and sensitively. They asked tentatively whether a special programme from the stricken town would be appropriate or welcome – not immediately, perhaps, but a few months down the line when people would be in a better state of mind to put their experiences into some sort

Checking a shot with jib cameraman,
Jeff Thomas, in All Saints Church,
Cockermouth.

of perspective. Churches Together in Cockermouth, an alliance representing all the Christian churches in the area, consulted together and said yes. After all, *Songs of Praise* was well known, much loved, and, crucially, trusted to be able to handle people's loss sensitively.

So it was that a special programme reflecting (and, after all the destruction, *celebrating*) the resilience, the cooperation, the selflessness, and the sheer human warmth of this close-knit community was broadcast on 21 February 2010.

What emerged was a portrait of a town united in hardship but determined to move forward together. On air the Revd Wendy Sanders, the Area Team Rector, was moved to tears when she spoke of the help that people had given each other in those disruptive times. She spoke of the simple human compassion of churchgoers and non-churchgoers alike as they opened their arms to everyone in need. The churches themselves had played a vital role in providing food, clothing, and accommodation for people whose homes had been flooded, while in the town centre Christ Church acted as a temporary support centre, housing Social Services, the Red Cross, and numerous non-official sources of help. The

finished programme reflected this, and framed the hardship and disruption with hymns that offered hope for the future: "O, for a Thousand Tongues to Sing"; "Brother, Sister, Let Me Serve You"; "Beauty for Brokenness"; "Lord of All Hopefulness"; "O God Our Help in Ages Past".

This was classic *Songs of Praise* and goes some way to explaining why the programme has endured for so long. It had come to a community as a welcome guest, not as a prying interloper. It had worked closely with local people, listening to their stories, recording their emotions, and crafting their shared calamity into a positive and uplifting experience. In so doing *Songs of Praise* had been uniquely privileged to share in people's lives and to be part of the healing process of an entire community. Yes, the scars were there – whether in the shape of the gigantic boulders littering the local sports field, or, more poignantly, in the washed-out shell that had been one woman's shop – but the mood was hopeful. And, as always, the people were the programme's strength. For *Songs of Praise* is nothing if not a people's programme, first and last. And it is people who have kept the programme alive for half a century, making it the longest running religious television programme in the world.

Those people have come from all walks of life, from pop stars to prime ministers (Margaret Thatcher, Tony Blair, Gordon Brown, David Cameron) and, on one occasion, the entire front bench and shadow cabinet in a special programme from the House of Commons. There have been unexpected appearances from entertainers such as Spike Milligan, Ken Dodd, Cliff Richard, and Chris de Burgh. Jo Brand showed her prowess on the church organ and Duncan Bannatyne from *Dragons' Den* talked about his relationship with God. All of which has helped to prove that *Songs of Praise* is not some churchy ghetto on the margins of the television schedules but a popular music programme accessible to all.

The programme has not been afraid to take risks with its guests. In 2009, for example, it courted controversy by featuring an interview with Garry Brotherston, a convicted murderer who was sentenced to life imprisonment for stabbing a man in a street brawl, and who served eleven years in Glasgow's Barlinnie Prison before

his release. The programme has featured many a saint, so why choose so obvious a sinner? The answer goes to the heart of what *Songs of Praise* is and does. First of all the programme chooses a location for a reason – not as an excuse to show pretty pictures. In this case it came to Scotland to commemorate the 200th anniversary of the Scottish Bible Society. Secondly, it comes by invitation, and thirdly, it does so to reflect the *entire* Christian community, not just a single section or denomination. The Scottish Bible Society is a resource for churches and people across the world, and it was appropriate to

Above: Members of the government and the opposition join together for a *Songs of Praise* from parliament.

Left: Comedienne Jo Brand.

Below: Sally Magnusson talks with the then Prime Minister Gordon Brown at 10 Downing Street.

Left: Cliff Richard talks to Pam Rhodes about what his faith means to him.

Bottom right: An ex-serviceman remembers fallen colleagues.

reflect its life-changing work in a special programme. It was also appropriate to feature people with interesting and unusual stories to tell. That meant, however controversial it would prove to be, featuring Garry Brotherston, who spoke of his own life-change in the form of repentance and conversion to Christianity while in jail. Crucially, however, he was not allowed a platform to speak unchallenged. He was interviewed by Sally Magnusson, a journalist by training, who probed deeply into his motivation to ensure that his story was not a sanitised rewriting of the facts but a genuine and universal message of personal transformation brought about by faith. Moreover the production team tracked down

Remembrance Day 1995

In 1995 the programme broadcast interviews with some ex-servicemen from Newcastle who had worked on the infamous Burma Railway, built by the Japanese using forced labour during the Second World War. Some of them had also been taken from the railway and sent to Japan to work alongside villagers in a mine.

At the end of the war the survivors built a wooden memorial in the village to those who had died. Forty years later they returned to Japan to discover that the wooden cross had been replaced by a more permanent memorial and that villagers laid flowers there every day. The emotion was palpable, prompting one man to say, "I can't forget but I can now forgive."

There is an equally moving postscript to the story. A lady watching the programme with her blind ex-RAF husband recognised on the restored memorial the name of her husband's brother, whose fate had been unknown for all those years. The team then put him in touch with the Geordie ex-soldiers and they were able to fill in the gaps of his brother's final days.

Top: An outside broadcast van at Clovelly in the early nineties.

Below left: Steve Chalke filming with Cliff Richard in Romania with cameraman Tom Ritchie (middle), director Simon Hammond (in cap), and soundman Mike Savage (with beard).

Below right: Pam Rhodes and friends are conducted by a local minister filming a special carols programme in Worth Valley, 1992.

the family of the man Brotherston had murdered and informed them in advance about the programme so that it would not come as a surprise.

Not all the *Songs of Praise* programmes, of course, are controversial. They can be light-hearted, such as the one built around the annual Bed Race in Knaresborough, featuring a team of vicars entering the race to raise money for a local hospice, or the programme marking the end of the long-running TV sitcom *Last of the Summer Wine*. *Songs of Praise* has been broadcast from the Blackpool

illuminations, from the pantomime, from the football stadium; it has featured jazz, rock, gospel, reggae, and swing, and has been equally at home on the seafront at Clovelly as in the nave of Canterbury Cathedral. For *Songs of Praise* goes where the people go, and has done for fifty memorable years.

"Songs of Praise *never stops changing.*"

Pamela Hossick, producer

It is the people who make the programme tick and the people who are the stars. Well, up to a point. For it is impossible to ignore the music, which shares top billing with the people. Or to put it another way, if the people are the heartbeat, the music is the breath. And one would not survive without the other.

The power of community hymn-singing is well described by Bob Prizeman, the programme's music adviser. "I remember at school being so thrilled to be part of the rising phrases in the Hallelujah chorus," he says, "and lending my pathetic voice to that crescendo. I vividly remember that feeling. So I know what a wonderful sensation people in the congregation are

experiencing. It's a mutually supportive thing and very powerful."

Former series producer Michael Wakelin goes even further. "I live on hymns. My faith is in hymns more than in Bible quotes and if I'm looking for reassurance and comfort in the storms of life I will turn to hymns to pull me through. And they mean more to me as I get older." But perhaps the former head of religious broadcasting, Colin Morris, summed it up most concisely when he said, "People can often sing what they cannot say."

This is all very well, but is *Songs of Praise* as committed to congregational hymn-singing today as it was when the first

programme was broadcast from Cardiff fifty years ago? Haven't spectaculars with the Red Arrows, singsongs at Old Trafford, and school choir competitions taken the programme off in an entirely different direction? No. For the Tabernacle Baptist Chapel is to Old Trafford and the Queen Elizabeth Hall what the acorn is to the oak: the two are different in their outward appearance but connected by a mysterious force that binds one inextricably to the other. To use another metaphor, *Songs of Praise* is always moving. If it had stood still it would have been overtaken and replaced. By being different it has stayed the same.

A sunny outdoor broadcast from Dartmouth in 2004.

GINNING NIGHT

WHAT'S MY LINE?

at 9.30

7.25
THE NEWS

7.30
THE KAY STARR ENGLISH MUSIC-HALL
featuring America's dynamic singing personality
KAY STARR
with
DERYCK GUYLER
JACK BILLINGS AND
GEORGE BARON
THE GALLOW GLASS
CEILI BAND
The Beryl Stott Singers
The Irving Davies Dancers
and
Woolf Phillips and his Orchestra
Dance director, Irving Davies
Script by BRAD ASHTON
Sets designed by Lionel Radford
Associate producer, Hal Stanley
Produced by RICHARD AFTON
BBC recording
See page 12

8.15
THE SUNDAY-NIGHT PLAY
presents
EMRYS JONES
PETRA DAVIES
BARRY LETTS
EDWARD WOODWARD
in
A Clean Kill
by MICHAEL GILBERT
with
Helen Christie
Laurence Hardy
Carmel McSharry
Produced by David J. Thomas
Cast in order of appearance:
Ann Patten..............PETRA DAVIES
Charles Reese...........EMRYS JONES
Hilda Reese.............HELEN CHRISTIE
Mrs. Turvey.............CARMEL McSHARRY
Mr. Schofield...........BARRY LETTS
Mr. Senior..............LAURENCE HARDY
Superintendent Morland
                        EDWARD WOODWARD
Police Constable..EIFION WYN JONES
Film cameraman, Russell Walker
Film editor, Douglas Mair
Designer, David Butcher
From Wales
BBC recording
The quarrel Hilda Reese had with her husband over the sale of his newly patented cleaning fluid had unexpected and even fatal results, but things took an even more serious turn when Superintendent Morland was called in to investigate.
See page 13

9.30
WHAT'S MY LINE?
Chairman,
Eamonn Andrews
Panel:
Isobel Barnett
Barbara Kelly
David Nixon
A Guest Panellist
and
a mystery guest celebrity
Research by Julia Cave
Directed by Sydney Lotterby
Produced by JOHN WARRINGTON
Devised by
Mark Goodson and Bill Todman
Televised by arrangement with CBS
and Maurice Winnick
See page 13

5
SUNDAY STORY
The Story of David
told by Cyril Fletcher
1: The Youngest Son
Script by CHAD VARAH
Produced by
JOHN ELPHINSTONE-FYFFE
BBC recording

6.10
THE NEWS

6.15
SONGS OF PRAISE
Congregational hymn-singing
from
TABERNACLE BAPTIST CHAPEL,
CARDIFF
with
Heather Harper (soprano)
Conducted by Mansel Thomas
Organist, V. Anthony Lewis
Introduced by
the Rev. Dr. Gwilym ap Robert
Produced by
GETHYN STOODLEY THOMAS
BBC recording
See page 12

6.55
MEETING POINT
Coping with Life
The Rev. Dr. Hugh Douglas
talks about pools, planets, pills
—and Providence
Produced by
the Rev. Dr. RONALD FALCONER
BBC recording
From Scotland

Cyril Fletcher

Tells the story of David in 'Sunday Story' this evening at 6.5

9.55
THE

10.5
JULI

sings
Love
on the
accompa
Henri
and h
The C
stage
Desig
Prod
BBC
See

10.3
TH
CO
Ker
dis
tha
Fr
of
As
Pr

10
T

A 1961 programme featured soloist Cy Grant. Here he is (top) with producer Gethyn Stoodley Thomas, production assistant Miss Margaret Price and organist Arwel Hughes; and below discussing the music with Arwel Hughes.

RE MY
CRET
e slim, like me

Left Bank

JULIETTE GRECO

★

I Maddox St.,
NAME
Block Capitals
ADDRESS

CHAPTER 1

1961–71: The First Ten Years

From accident to design

To look at a copy of the *Radio Times* from 1961 and read the early evening BBC television schedule for Sunday 1 October is to enter a vanished broadcasting world the like of which will never return.

At 6.05 p.m. the *Sunday Story*, scripted by the Revd Chad Varah, an Anglican priest who had founded the Samaritans a few years earlier, featured the life of the biblical King David read by the popular English comedian of the time, Cyril Fletcher (catchphrase: "Pin back your lugholes"). At 6.15 the very first edition of *Songs of Praise* was billed without fanfare or fuss, and was followed by *Meeting Point*, another product of the BBC religion department and a cross between today's *Question*

Time and *The Moral Maze*. This particular edition featured the Revd Dr Hugh Douglas expounding the theme of "pools, planets, pills, and Providence" and was itself followed by three hours of drama and light entertainment. A ten-minute preview of the Labour Party Conference in Blackpool brought us back to everyday life with a bump before the *Epilogue*, with its "prayers for the family", took us to close-down at 10.55. And that was it. By eleven o'clock, its cocoa drunk, the nation was in its pyjamas fast asleep.

To understand religion's relative dominance of the evening's output it is important to remember that this was the era of the "closed period" when, by unofficial gentlemen's agreement, the Sunday evening schedule from 6.00-ish to around 7.30 was closed to all but

religious programmes (popularly known as the "God Slot"). If such an arrangement seems quaint in our multi-channel era, remember too, that it was only five years earlier that the so-called "Toddlers' Truce" had ended: the agreement under which both BBC and ITV (then the country's only two television channels) shut down their transmitters between 6.00 and 7.00 to allow the nation's children to be put to bed without tears or tantrums.

The suggestion that a new-fangled programme of hymn-singing should go out on Sunday evening was at first fiercely resisted – ironically not by the news and current affairs directorate or similar high-minded vested interests but by the BBC's very own religious broadcasting department, which argued that this would be

Right: Filming on the Rio Grande in 1987.

Below: A cameraman perches on top of a phone box in order to get just the right shot.

lowering the tone of religious programming. The producers responsible for *Meeting Point* put their case forcefully, arguing that the high intellectual standards of theological enquiry they had been pioneering in televised discussions and documentaries risked being undercut by this popular and really rather vulgar forty minutes of community song. Impassioned debate ensued within the department and angry threats were directed at the controller of BBC television, Stuart Hood, and his assistant, Donald Baverstock (a key player in the *Songs of Praise* story, as you will shortly see). Hood dug in his heels and threatened to give the programme to light entertainment if religion didn't like it. That did the trick. With grudging acceptance from the religious broadcasting department, *Songs of Praise* was born.

Getting the shot (1)

Tom Ritchie is a cameraman who embodies all the qualities of the *Songs of Praise* technical crew: superb professionalism, adaptability, and a commitment to giving (and getting) the best. In 1996, filming in Svalbard in the Arctic Circle in temperatures of minus 20°C, he excelled himself with a series of stunning landscape panoramas that took the producer's breath away. Then, during a late-night meal in the hotel, he felt the light was perfect for an even better shot (they were, of course, making the programme during the annual six months of daylight). As he got up to go outside, the team's Norwegian fixer said, "I'll come with you."

"No need," said Tom. "You carry on with your meal."

"No, I'll join you," he insisted.

"Really," said Tom, "I'll be fine."

"Not necessarily," the Norwegian continued, reaching for his rifle. "Polar bears."

Strangely enough Tom relented. After an hour the two returned with even more stunning pictures in the can – and not a shot fired. But, as Tom agreed, you can never be too careful.

Right: Disguising a camera as a bush.

Top: David Baverstock, who first came up with the idea for *Songs of Praise*.

Bottom: The Crystal Palace transmitter as it looked in 1956.

the singing. "Here," he said, "were ordinary people in their best hats singing with their souls."

Straightaway he decided that such a programme could have wide popular appeal on the BBC. Not only that, he is said to have reasoned, a Sunday evening slot would mean that the OB units that were lying idle after Saturday's football and racing transmissions could be economically redeployed at churches, chapels, and other non-sporting venues.

The idea went down well. Baverstock was fêted as second only

The story of how Donald Baverstock (who is generally credited with the original idea for *Songs of Praise*) decided that a programme of hymn-singing would be a welcome addition to the BBC's output has been told before. But it misses, perhaps, an important dimension which is rarely, if ever, mentioned.

The story goes that Baverstock, a talented producer with a keen appreciation of popular programming (without his weekday news and current affairs programme *Tonight*, there could have been no *Nationwide* or *One Show*), was visiting the Crystal Palace transmitter when he caught sight of a recording of Welsh hymn-singing. A "homesick Welshman" himself he was immediately entranced by what he described as "the wholehearted and uninhibited quality" of

SONGS of PRAISE

to Einstein or Marie Curie and the programme idea was put in motion. What is missing from this eureka moment, however, is the fact that a popular hymn-singing programme already existed on the BBC and had been attracting enthusiastic audiences for over twenty years since 1940. Its title was *Sunday Half Hour*, and it had apparently slipped under the TV radar (not unusually) because it was broadcast on *radio*.

So much has changed since then that it is fruitless to rehearse the latent antagonisms between the two media or to argue the relative merits of each. Suffice it to say that twenty years of successfully transmitting hymns into the homes of appreciative listeners to the wireless must have convinced somebody somewhere that *televising* congregational hymns might not be quite as daft as certain parties had first suggested. In short, *Songs of Praise* was now in business.

St Paul's Church in Colwyn Bay, Malone Presbyterian Church in Belfast, and St John's Kirk in Perth were among the first to play host to the corporation's OBs, and interest was gradually generated further afield. As the decade wore on, churches, chapels, tabernacles, abbeys, and cathedrals were all anxious to be featured – not to mention schools, hospitals, prisons, coalmines, holiday camps, and concert halls.

By the standards of today's technology the early programmes were probably static and

First mentioned in 1126, St John's Kirk. is the oldest building in Perth, Scotland. It was the site of a famous sermon against idolatry delivered by John Knox during the Reformation in 1559.

In June 1943, Prime Minister Winston Churchill gives the "V" sign outside 10 Downing Street, London.

uninventive. I say "probably" because few of them survive and we have to rely on the memories of the people who watched them to recreate the experience. What is known for sure, however, is that the equipment needed to record and broadcast them was heavy, bulky, and relatively inflexible and would inevitably have restricted variety in the shooting. We also know that at that time TV lights were not equipped with dimmers and, when switched on, became incredibly hot – so much so that at the first rehearsal at the Tabernacle Chapel in Cardiff the congregation had to take a breather for twenty minutes to allow the lamps to be switched off and to cool down.

Baverstock admitted that the programmes had little to offer visually except close-ups of faces, so it is probably fair to assume that from week to week the look of the programme changed little. Even so producers and directors could rise to grand occasions – such as the broadcast from Harrow School on the death of Winston Churchill in 1965 – and mount moving and powerful set pieces.

The presenter Geoffrey Wheeler remembers this occasion well. "I was presenting a live record show on the *Light Programme* between 8.00 and 10.00 in the morning. Halfway through, the producer

SONGS OF PRAISE AND PRAYERS

came on to me in the headphones and said, 'Don't do any more announcements. Churchill's died. We want you up in Harrow now.'" The programme was taken off air as soon as possible and replaced with a solemn announcement and an obituary. Meanwhile Geoffrey was on the Metropolitan Line, rushing off to the great man's old school where an OB unit was already in place and on standby in anticipation of an event that had been expected for some time.

It was a live programme, replacing the recorded *Songs of Praise* for that week, and it established Geoffrey, who by now was a regular presenter of the programme, as a safe pair of hands in a crisis. His mellifluous baritone blended authority with warmth and framed the programme perfectly for a nation gradually coming to terms with its loss. As usual he linked the hymns faultlessly, explaining how they had come to be written and why they were apt as a commemoration of Churchill's life.

By the mid-1960s a template for the programme had been created and, week by week, producers pretty much stuck to it. Geoffrey would prepare a few words setting the scene, giving the history of the church and any unusual or otherwise interesting facts about the place; then he would introduce the first hymn. After that he would cue up the next hymn by explaining something about its meaning and the circumstances under which it had been written, and carry on the same way for the rest of the programme, varying the introduction only slightly by announcing before the penultimate hymn that a prayer and blessing would be given by the Revd X, vicar of the featured church.

"People were kind enough to write in to me saying my links

Right: Geoffrey Wheeler chats to the floor manager in the early 1960s, just before going on air in Nantwich.

the programme and that is what it will always be. There's no other show like it around the world." But we digress. Let us return to the broadcasting landscape fifty years ago when *Songs of Praise* was in its infancy.

Although this was the 1960s, the "swinging" tag was definitely not to be applied to the religious broadcasting department. Most of the staff were men and many of these were ordained ministers or priests. Even Geoffrey Wheeler felt it important to let it be discreetly known to his *Songs of Praise* audience that he himself was a lay reader in the church. On one occasion, when a live worship programme was coming from his parish church in Cheshire, he thought it right to be filmed in his reader's robes reading the Gospel from the pulpit.

But if Geoffrey was (and is) a devout churchman he was also (and remains) a consummate professional. He remembers one occasion during a *Songs of Praise* rehearsal (though diplomatically forgetting the name of the church) when a young curate was becoming visibly irritated by Geoffrey's (faultless) linking script. Unable to contain his irritation any longer the young man stood up in his pew and, pointing at a by now baffled presenter, shouted out in front of crew and congregation: "This is

were like a mini sermon," Geoffrey remembers. "In fact what I was doing was the reverse of what, say, Charles Wesley had done. His writing method was to take a large theme and condense it into four perfect lines whereas what I was doing was taking those four lines and reconstituting them into a minute and a half's worth of introduction."

With its church location and prayer and blessing at the end, the programme had the liturgical feel of a religious service. But, while there was a sense of reverence and decorum appropriate to the place, the programme had not been conceived of as an act of worship.

Even today one of the persistent misunderstandings surrounding the programme is that it is designed to replicate a church service. It is not. It is, in essence, a Christian music programme. Its current executive producer, Tommy Nagra, would be a rich man if he had a pound for every time he has had to clarify this – whether, on occasion, to its loyal core audience or, more frequently, to the "phantom" audience that has a fixed and erroneous opinion of what the programme is, based on a couple of programmes they *think* they may have seen some time in the 1960s. "This is a musical celebration of the Christian faith," says Tommy. "That is the DNA of

Presenter Sally Magnusson interviewing Prince Charles in the Castle of Mey, the late Queen Mother's home, September 2005.

Sally Magnusson

Favourite hymns:
"Be Thou My Vision",
"O, Love That Wilt Not Let Me Go".

"What I felt right from the beginning is that *Songs of Praise* is about people. I've always taken exception to the idea that it's about *ordinary* people, because they are nearly always extraordinary people. Long before television got into reality shows, *Songs of Praise* was going into communities and celebrating what mattered in people's lives. In the days when I was stuck in a news studio conducting conversations and stewarding argy-bargies with politicians I really appreciated getting out into small villages, being welcomed into people's houses over tea and scones, and really getting in touch with people and their lives. And you got a sense that you were tapping into stories and issues that were really not being discussed elsewhere. So I've always loved it as an antidote to the frenetic world of news and current affairs, but at the same time keeping in touch with some of the deeper things that really matter in life. And on occasions such as the Gulf War or Dunblane you are also conscious that you are marking something important in the life of the nation.

It's the democratic nature of the programme I've always appreciated. Anyone and everyone can appear on it from royalty to the local postman and they all know they can feel safe."

ridiculous. I should be doing this. Not him!" The vicar intervened, but the curate was having none of it. "I'm ordained and he isn't," he went on. The outburst was doubtless a cry from the heart, but it did not enhance the mood. In the end the vicar asked him to leave and normality returned. "But he had completely missed the point," says Geoffrey charitably. "This was not a church service and I was not pretending to be ordained. Being a curate is having a vocation. That's quite different from being a professional presenter paid to do a job of work. I wasn't there to preach but I was there to be enthusiastic – and to know which camera was focusing on me at any one time and be ready for it."

During the first ten years of its life *Songs of Praise* was produced by teams in the different BBC regions with producers and directors whose first love might not always have been religion. They were generalists who were given production assignments that may have taken them one week to the Cheltenham Festival, the next to the Cup Final, and the next to an abbey church in Northumberland for a *Songs of Praise*.

For many of them it was just another job, and they brought to it greater or lesser degrees of sensitivity and understanding. As a result the programmes lacked any overall consistency and identity. And that, in the eyes of one man who was to play a pivotal role in the development of *Songs of Praise*, was a grave weakness that could, in the long term, prove fatal to the programme. Changes needed to be made, and Raymond Short (who sadly died while this book was in production) was the man to make them.

After service in the RAF toward the end of the Second World War, Ray had studied theology at Cambridge before being ordained as a Methodist minister in 1953. He had trained as an architect and had an eye for shape and balance. Above all, perhaps, he had an encyclopedic knowledge of hymns, which he referred to as "the church's folk music", and could expound extempore on their provenance and deeper meaning. All a junior colleague needed to say was "Love Divine, All Loves Excelling" for Ray to reply unprompted, "Number 431 in the *Methodist Hymn Book*." "There is a Green Hill Far Away?" "Number 180." And so on. (The hymn-book was revised in 1983 and republished under the title *Hymns and Psalms*, meaning that the above hymns are now numbers 267 and 178 respectively. Ray would have known that, too.)

It is often said that the Methodist Church was "born in song". If so, then Ray was a worthy inheritor of the Wesleyan musical tradition. Indeed Andrew Barr, Ray's protégé and successor, believes that, denominationally, *Songs of Praise* is, at root, Methodist, whether that was the original intention or not. He points out that in the nineteenth century many Methodists would carry hymn-books in their pockets ready to spring into song and to deploy, on request, an appropriate verse or two that might accompany the sorrows or celebrations of their neighbours' important life-events.

Researcher Valetta Stallabrass.

"Its longevity is due to its audience."

Valetta Stallabrass, former researcher

"Some Methodists thought I was a renegade and had given up the ministry to work in TV. But it wore off. Songs of Praise was part of my ministry."

Ray Short, Methodist minister and first series producer

Ray knew the value of congregational hymn-singing instinctively. "Essentially the purpose of hymns is to express the corporate response of a community," he wrote in a memo of the time. "Hymns are meant to enable a lot of people to share in proclaiming their faith. The right hymn for a particular occasion is one that reflects and resonates within the minds and hearts of the singers." How many producers, fresh from filming Aston Villa vs Notts Forest on Saturday, would have been similarly attuned to the deeper exigences of *Songs of Praise* on Sunday? And how many would have written (as Ray did) in post-programme notes, "The hymn is the most undervalued weapon in the armoury of the Christian church. In these religiously disastrous times it is vital that we

understand how hymns work, what makes a good hymn, and how to use them to the full"?

Watching *Songs of Praise* in the late 1960s he concluded that insufficient numbers of outside broadcast directors had grasped the subtlety of the raw material they were handling. "Cameramen were shooting at random," he recalls. "A shot of three people here, two people there. Two kids fighting over who should hold the hymn-book and even once a shot of a bird that had flown into Liverpool Cathedral. Hopeless."

Most of the broadcasts were adequate, some were outstanding, and some poor, largely because all the regions had their own ways of doing things. "What I was trying to do was make a random selection of programmes into a unified whole," he says, before adding bluntly, "What I had to do was make *Songs of Praise* look like a series. Before that it had looked like a series of accidents."

Little in the way of extra resources was required. All it needed was an ear for the music and an eye for the visual shot that naturally accompanied and complemented it. Ray had both. His time had come and he was made the first *Songs of Praise* series producer in 1970.

He soon introduced changes – changes which have remained to

Getting the shot (2)

The Witney Feast is an annual Oxfordshire fair with its origins in the thirteenth century. These days it plays host to a traditional funfair attracting showmen and women from all over the country, and in 1988 it was the location for a special *Songs of Praise* programme produced by Chris Mann. He had lined up a complex opening shot involving presenter Sally Magnusson sitting on a carousel galloper cueing up an orchestra which was out of sight behind her. As the merry-go-round rotated, the orchestra would come into view and the programme would begin. After several takes Chris decided the shot lacked something. Then he realised that the fairground ride behind the carousel was not moving. "Fill it up with people and get it started," he said, and set up the shot again. It was a stunning opening sequence but, aware that they were now overrunning their schedule, he quickly moved on to the next. Only after half an hour did he realise that the ride was still turning – with its occupants by now turning an alarming shade of green. The ride was stopped and the volunteers were let off – distinctly unimpressed by Chris's attention to detail.

ABOUT THE NORTH

Sunday's Songs of Praise comes from the Metropolitan Cathedral of Christ the King, Liverpool, and is introduced by Geoffrey Wheeler.
Here Vernon Noble talks to producer RAYMOND SHORT, the man responsible for

Religious Broadcasting in the North

IT's a special kind of man who can speak of religion and entertainment in the same breath. Ray Short, for example, Religious Broadcasting Organiser for BBC North, a parson who rarely wears his distinctive collar—'for one thing, it's not very comfortable'—is the instigator and producer of a great variety of radio and television programmes which reflect the thoughts and needs of our time.

'We have to be entertaining,' he says, and he broadly interprets the word in the relationship of a host to his guest. When you entertain *somebody* in your home you try to satisfy

his requirements, to cater for his particular tastes, to provide enlivening conversation.

That is the way he looks at it—broadcasting as a communication, whether through a straight talk, a radio magazine like *Calendar*, the relay of a church service and *Songs of Praise*, or television programmes such as his folk-music competition *Grief and Glory* and *The Youthful Eye*.

Ray Short's enthusiasm for the medium includes the mechanics of it. The techniques fascinate him, either work in the studio or filming out and about in the North or as part of a team of twenty or so for the outside

television broadcast from Liver politan Cathedral on Palm Sur phones and cameras are the too fession.

It looked at one time as if the been set squares and slide rules at Liverpool University's Schoo ture, but after four years' service his interests took another d studied theology at Cambridge a Methodist Minister, first in Hun at South Shields and Durham.

While in South Shields he weekly column to the local even *Gazette*, and in Durham he or sessions for prisoners in the ga stimulating thing I ever did.'

Then in 1961 he joined the chester as Religious Broadcast and was appointed head of th four years later—the first Meth occupy the post. Now he doesn't self as denominational. He hat

He sums up his outlook by sort of people I find I have mo with are radical Christians.'

The wide variety of programm Ray Short and his staff deal listeners and viewers who are b of church—and he never shrin controversial. 'I have always w people who don't share my views to make religion understood eve agree with it. Part of our jo find ways of awakening people issues, to get them to ask relig because until they do that ther giving religious answers.'

And he says all this as a ma cerned about the state of the c and also as a technician wh demonstrate Christianity in act be afraid of opinions which may who are cosily sitting in their p everybody who appreciated th boys and girls in *The Youthful* startling to hear Cliff Richard *of Praise* in a modern idiom.

Ray Short is very close to probably because—at forty-thr at heart himself, with a youth a youthful energy. He unders pathises with this generation' criticisms. He plays a roaring tennis, and golf when he can painting is one of his main landscape artist himself and in work.

His office walls are gay with a cartoon entitled *Dig this* vicars uprooting a tree) to mo jects and a coloured drawing sonable tiger by his nine-year-one of his three children.

When Ray Short exchang studio, cameras, and control out to explore new territory i religion. He strides briskly coveries, exploiting the visu

A community broadcast from Eastbourne, September 1985.

this day. In the early programmes, for example, the whole event was centred on a church, a chapel, a school, or some other self-contained location. This arrangement had the advantage of being able to deliver a ready-made congregation. But for Ray this was too restricting. Hymns, he believed, are about community. Accordingly he insisted that any *Songs of Praise* programme from then on had to be a collaborative, ecumenical event. Certainly, the people would be filmed in one church (probably the most photogenic church in the town), but the venue had to play host to all the other local Christians from churches, chapels, schools, and fellowships in the vicinity.

So, if you wrote to him asking for *Songs of Praise* to come and help your church celebrate its 400th anniversary, for example, and to film the congregation having a jolly good time, you were told by return that this idea was a non-starter. Only if the town or village met as one, put aside its denominational differences for a week or so, and came together in joint Christian celebration would *Songs of Praise* even consider turning up. Towns and villages quickly got the message and approved of it.

This simple yet radical idea proved to be a tonic for Christian communities across the country and soon they were queueing up to take part. Whatever alchemy Ray worked on-screen (more of which later), the immediate effect off-screen was that men and women living within miles – or sometimes yards – of each other but who had never really spoken became friends and collaborators. This was a community enterprise whose effects would live on long after the cameras had left. And while the programme could be endlessly dissected at review meetings and its impact assessed in terms of audience figures, the effect the experience had on actual communities – on real people rather than broadcasting statistics – was incalculable.

Once a location had been selected Ray circulated a check-list of requirements that he had drawn up in advance. In it he first outlined the programme's intention: to let the viewer share in the local community's celebration of its faith. Next he suggested the formation of a small local committee which would, among other things, advise

Bottom: Filming in Sherborne Abbey in December 1996.

Right: An Easter service from Winchester Cathedral.

on the composition of the choirs and nominate a conductor and organist to direct the music in collaboration with the BBC team.

This last suggestion was the only latent flaw in the overall scheme. As later producers would eventually discover, putting the musical content completely in the hands of the available local talent and conferring musical control on local organists and conductors had inherent weaknesses which would eventually be tested to breaking point. For the moment, though, the structure held and Ray moved swiftly on to the nuts and bolts of the televised broadcast.

He made it clear that on the night everyone should be prepared for a full rehearsal before the final recording, a demanding but vital requirement which called for stamina and patience. He also urged forbearance in the days beforehand, warning that the BBC's workers would be tramping about the church carting scaffolding, lighting, cabling, and cameras – those minor technical bits and pieces without which nothing would get on the air. "Our men are very used to this operation," he wrote, "and when they leave, it is as if they have never been."

Good as he was at coordinating the logistics off-screen, Ray was an acknowledged master of combining sound and picture on-screen to make a satisfying televisual experience that could make both more than the sum of their individual parts. "The initial problem facing the TV director is to take a sea of faces and a sea of noise and make it seem inevitable that those featured on-screen should be in shot at that particular moment," he explained, before adding with characteristic understatement, "It's harder than it looks."

To accomplish this he drew on his own native strengths – the painter's eye for form and composition and the Methodist minister's ear for music and song. It also helped that he knew the hymn-book backwards:

I'd take every hymn and give it a visual rhythmic pattern. I felt that every hymn lent itself to a certain visual treatment. So, for example, "Onward Christian Soldiers" would suggest group shots. I'd get the cameraman to focus on three or four or six faces in fairly pacey succession whereas if the hymn was "Just as I Am" we'd need an entirely different approach. That is an intensely personal hymn, so focusing on four people would make no sense at all because no one would know which individual was having that experience

Ray Short, a keen artist, holds up one of his paintings.

at that moment. For that hymn you needed to focus on one face at a time.

For cameramen used to focusing on penalties, free kicks, and corners this was a skill waiting to be acquired. Ever the patient pastor Ray took it upon himself to introduce it gently but firmly to his film crews and to let it be known to regional producers what he expected the house style to be.

The new gizmo of the age, for example, was the zoom lens, a brilliant device for homing in on the Cruft's champion schnauzer or the photo-finish at Kempton Park, but something to be used with restraint on *Songs of Praise*. So, at rehearsal, when Ray would instruct a camera to zoom in on a particular face, his instruction would be perfectly timed to coincide with the beat of the music being played and the meaning of the verse being sung. The cameraman, by contrast, might be recalling his prize-winning close-up of a slide tackle at White Hart Lane the previous week and interpret Ray's instruction as a cue to zoom in from wide angle to close-up in a split second.

Again, Ray patiently explained the feel of the hymn to the cameramen in order that they could close in at an appropriately gentle pace. They learned quickly and appreciated the instruction. Indeed one engineering manager remarked to Ray's wife, Katharine, that he liked to get his men (invariably men in those days) on to one of Ray's programmes soon after they had joined the unit because he was good with them and taught them all sorts of techniques – and, incidentally, in his capacity as Methodist minister, married a fair few of them over the years, too.

With the exception of his final programme Ray never wore his dog collar on set, but he was constantly aware of his ministerial vocation. For him his work in religious broadcasting was simply another arm of his ministry and, as a consequence, there was no discrepancy between his being a minister and being a director of programmes. His meticulously planned shots were not for his own self-aggrandisement (though he took a proper sense of pride in his professionalism) but essentially for transmitting a spiritual message: "I wanted the viewer to take seriously what the hymns were all about. They were about God. And I wanted the congregation to be filmed singing reflectively about what God meant to them. An ugly shot could ruin an entire sequence and destroy the programme."

An early programme that underlined the need for such sensitivity was the one broadcast in May 1967 from the Afan Lido Sports Centre just seven months after a colliery spoil-heap had collapsed, sliding into the village of Aberfan in South Wales and killing 144 people, 116 of them children. There was intense debate in the office about the appropriateness of a programme with the word "praise" in its title but, after sensitive approaches had been made, it was clear that local churches welcomed the opportunity to take part in what would become a televised memorial to the dead. It also gave viewers an insight into how the community was dealing with loss and bereavement and into the various ways in which faith was helping them carry on.

In this, and in every other programme since, the *Songs of Praise* team's commitment to the off-screen experience was central. Producers were encouraged never to lose sight of the value of the day-to-day interaction of different Christian communities coming together in a common enterprise. As Ray Short put it, "We took some care to make it clear that this was an ecumenical event but we tried to do it naturally. It wasn't as if we were thumping a tub."

A tub-thumper Ray never was. His natural and ever respectful manner brought out the best in congregation and crew alike, who would forgive him for putting them through all the necessary rehearsal hours. At least, *most* would. "One priest got up in a rehearsal at St James's Piccadilly (in central London) and complained that we were making him rehearse something he did every Sunday," Ray remembers. "I had to explain that a televised programme was a different animal altogether from a Sunday service and that what I was doing was merely designed to make things look right on-screen." This last observation goes to the heart of what *Songs of Praise* does each week and explains partly why the programme has survived so long – making the ordinary look interesting and the everyday *entertaining*. Entertainment has never been something for which the programme has felt the need to apologise. On the contrary, it is its entertainment value that keeps it alive for millions of viewers every week. The simple truth is that no one will watch a dull programme, and it is equally true that what was entertaining in 1961 would not necessarily prove to be so ten years later as styles changed and audience expectation evolved. By the late 1970s this was precisely the dilemma that *Songs of Praise* faced. It was losing audiences in the face of competition from ITV, and something needed to be done to give the programme a sharper edge. The programme wasn't broken but it did need fixing. And these repairs were to give it an entirely new lease of life.

Aberfan coal tip avalanche, 1966. Rescuers fill sandbags and lay them on the coal tip above the flattened Pantglas Junior School to divert the spring that may have triggered the avalanche, entombing some 200 people. A huge mound of coal slag and sludge collapsed onto the Welsh mining village, killing 116 children and 28 adults.

CHAPTER 2

1971–85: Songs of Praise *Comes of Age*

> "Songs of Praise *is outside the normal run of programmes. It's a window on the world."*
>
> **Andrew Barr, former series producer**

The big makeover

The first decade of *Songs of Praise* had been a tremendous success. The programme was much loved, immensely popular, and recognised by millions as a fixed point in their Sunday evening viewing. Week by week viewers would gather in front of the screen, often singing along to the hymns, and enjoying an experience that could compensate, in some cases, for non-attendance at their local church.

Indeed then as now the phrase "I don't go to church but I do watch *Songs of Praise*" became a popular refrain well known to world-weary vicars trying to swell their slowly diminishing congregations.

But, as the 1960s gave way to the 1970s, the format of the programme was judged by some younger staff members to be in need of refreshment. It was holding its own in the ratings but, with increasing competition from ITV, how long could this

state of affairs be guaranteed? The old-style programme continued until the middle of the new decade when, under the management of Peter Armstrong, the new head of religious television broadcasting, *Songs of Praise* was dramatically reinvented.

An accomplished documentary film-maker himself, Armstrong pioneered innovations that were to alter the programme for good and make it, substantially, the

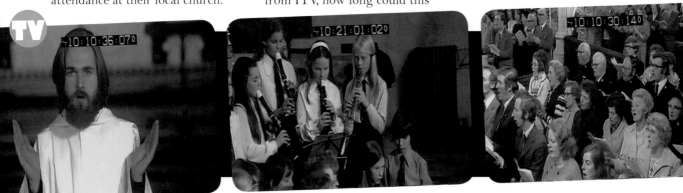

programme that it is today. With his background in current-affairs television, he decided that *Songs of Praise* needed a more journalistic edge. Yes, it had to have the hymns, but also more about the lives of the people selecting them. Audiences, he judged, were becoming tired of watching a hymn then a link, a hymn then a link and would be more inclined to watch if the programme could also tell the strong, personal stories of ordinary people that he felt sure were waiting to be told. Some existing staff were resentful toward the proposed changes and felt they would never work. Others were more enthusiastic and actively embraced the challenge. Either way, the change was going to be made.

A pilot programme was assembled involving the talents of, among others, Bill Nicholson – who would go on to establish himself as a Hollywood screen writer, with films such as *Gladiator*, starring Russell Crowe, and *Shadowlands*, starring Anthony Hopkins, among his writing credits. In 1977, however, with those achievements some way off, he would have to be content with filming the local people of Godmanchester in Huntingdonshire making jam

The new 'Songs of Praise': for better or worse?

THERE MUST be many who, like my wife and I, are unable to go out to church any longer and have appreciated *Songs of Praise* (Sundays BBC1) because we have felt ourselves one with the congregation in its worship.

The new set-up has completely destroyed this for us. Dodging in and out of the church to have a chat with first one person and then another has meant we no longer join in an act of worship. The BBC has largely removed congregational worship from its Sunday morning programme; is it to go from the evening as well?

Please restore the old set-up.

G. C. Matthews
Sheffield

Great relief
The 'new-look' *Songs of Praise* was a great relief to me as I was afraid that, vying for popularity, you would make it more secular or spectacular. It was an improvement – more meaningful, just what we need . . .

(Mrs) Beatrice Bewes
Lyndhurst, Hampshire

More contact
Congratulations on the new form of presentation of *Songs of Praise*.

I have often wondered about the folk when the camera picks them up in the congregation (I once saw a friend whom I had not seen for many years).

I now feel we have a little more contact with, at least, some of them and can think of them as individuals who live ordinary lives as I do.

(Mrs) H. Bradley
London, N21

No Wheeler?
I am bitterly disappointed that Geoffrey Wheeler is no longer with us for *Songs of Praise*. After all, 'getting through' to the few is surely *far* more important than pleasing the masses and beating ITV figures? Please bring him back to us soon.

(Mrs) Dorothy M. Heath
Heswall, Merseyside

That new tune
While I admire the new improved format of *Songs of Praise*, I really must protest at the new signature tune. What was wrong with the previous arrange-

ment whereby the church organist played something appropriate? The electronic jingle does nothing to update the programme.

John Boynton
Kidderminster,
Worcestershire

RAYMOND SHORT, Producer, 'Songs of Praise,' replies: *Songs of Praise* has been running since 1961 – and has become something of an institution. It is always difficult, and dangerous, to tamper with institutions, but we felt it was time to try to enrich the programme without cheapening it. In the new format the viewer is introduced to some of the people providing the singing. The local Christians are allowed to speak for themselves. We believe this creates a programme that is more religious as well as better television.

The hymn singing and the prayer and blessing retain the element of worship, and remain much the major part of the programme. Michael Barratt has joined the team of introducers, which still includes Geoffrey Wheeler.

Over the years Songs of Praise has maintained its wide audience. We are not primarily involved in a battle for ratings. But neither are we ashamed of wanting as many people as possible to watch a programme which expresses the real faith of ordinary Christians in words and music.

Definitely not diminutive

I was most interested in *Pale Hands I Loved* (12 January Radio 4), that particular Indian Love Lyric being very familiar to me as a child. There was, however, one error in the narrative.

In 1928, as a schoolgirl, I attended a recital in Bedford Corn Exchange to hear Dame Clara Butt and her husband, R. Kennerley Rumford. The latter was definitely not a 'diminutive figure' as stated in this broadcast.

On first appearing they both looked so splendid in evening dress that there was an audible gasp from the audience!

(Miss) Isobel B. Meikle
Glasgow

H. COLIN DAVIS, writer, 'Pale Hands I Loved,' replies:
I must have been about ten years old when I saw them in the Assembly Rooms at Malvern, I suppose, 55 years later, the memory can become distorted; but to a child that voice and that presence dwarfed all around it.

Hatherley and the critics

The Emigrants producer, Frank Hatherley, must have sighed with relief at some positive response to his enterprise (LETTERS, 1-7 January). Before he allows himself too much gratification, let me assure him that this viewer, and I believe many others, agreed absolutely with the critics' reaction . . .

Mr Hatherley implies that the critics' adverse reaction was just snobbery in the face of ordinary people living ordinary lives: in which case, why their approval for series like *Z Cars*, *Softly, Softly*, *When the Boat Comes In*, etc? And as for judging the quality of *any* programme, let alone drama, by its mass appeal, well, if he'll pardon the expression, *Crossroads*.

N. P. G. Wurr
London, SW4

FRANK HATHERLEY replies: *Mr Wurr declares himself on the side of the critics: such is his privilege.*

Detailed audience survey reports are now coming in. Part One of The Emigrants 'appealed strongly' to the great majority of its 9.25 million viewers who 'rated its story of ordinary, everyday people attempting to face up to today's problems as something new and different'. The characters were 'naturally portrayed' and their situation and environment was 'typical'.

Against that, the critics complained that the Parker family were 'the kind of people we should be

Debbie Thrower

Favourite hymns:
"The Love of My Lord is the
Essence", "Dear Lord and
Father of Mankind".

"It's real people, isn't it? It gives a voice to people you wouldn't normally hear in the general run of things on prime-time television. The other thing that's very important when you're watching it at home is that you get a lingering look at people, and they are just like your neighbours down the street. So if you're not from a Christian background and you're wondering what Christianity is all about and whether it is something you could be part of, you would look at these lovely faces and think, 'Yes, I could, because they're just like me and everybody else I know.'

And there is a real ecumenical feel about the programme. It's such a wonderful window on Christian communities at home and abroad. And even the shortest of interviews can be incredibly powerful.

The programme has affected my faith a great deal because I've become a Reader in the Church of England and I've taken on a chaplaincy role to older people just up the road from where I live. So *Songs of Praise* has been a very, very significant milestone along my journey of faith."

and sweeping the church. The team's effort was not deemed a complete success, and a few more attempts were made to knock the new format into shape before the new-look *Songs of Praise* eventually went out in 1977 from the Sussex town of Rye on Romney Marsh.

Perhaps the biggest single innovation in an already revamped programme was the appointment of Liz Gort as the permanent full-time researcher. Hitherto the few interviewees who had featured in the early programmes had all been suggested or vetted by the local clergy or by hastily convened local committees. With no real idea of what would make good television, vicars and ministers tended to plump automatically for the stalwarts of their congregations, the churchwardens and the flower-arrangers, the Sunday school teachers and the Mothers' Union volunteers – not all of whom had the most dramatic stories to tell.

The appointment of Liz changed all that. The brief was simple: to spend a week in any one place and ferret out the interesting people with the interesting stories. It was a licence to be inquisitive, but not to pry. Inevitably Liz would receive a list of the great and the good from the vicar, but she prided herself on being able to explore off-piste and to hunt out other people whose tales were not only

The red-tiled rooftops of Rye, seen from the tower of St Mary's Church, East Sussex.

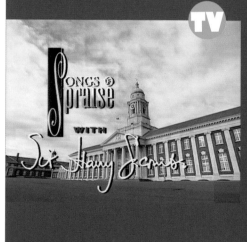

being broadcast on television for the first time, but in some cases were being told for the first time as well, sometimes surprising even the tellers. Liz's method was simple.

"I just used to hang about," she says, "following up suggestions by a person's friends and friends of friends." Spending a week in one place, incidentally, would be a luxury unheard of to Janis Knox, Lisa Ashton, or Judith Sharp, three of the programme's current researchers, who have to work to much tighter schedules than those of old – but who, week after week, still come up with the goods under enormous pressure. If you want an octogenarian who has moved from Britain to the Middle East to do his bit for peace in the region, just ask Janis. She will secure you one. In the appreciative (and incredulous) words of the executive producer, Tommy Nagra, "How do they find these people?" It is all part of the researcher's art, and one that was in its infancy when Liz Gort made the job her own in 1977.

One of the first interviewees Liz

SONGS OF PRAISE

had secured was the local postman, Ralph Holland. His story was simple but had the heartfelt quality that a good researcher knows instinctively will translate well into television. Mr Holland had had, he said with very English restraint, an unhappy childhood, but had come into contact with a kindly minister who, sensing the young man's unease with life, had taken Ralph under his wing and introduced him to his family. Without any pressure, he continued, he became a member of the Methodist Church and learned to love the hymns, in particular "Love Divine, All Loves Excelling", which, even at that distance from his childhood, never failed to remind him of the love and care that had been shown to him.

To illustrate the sequence, it was decided to follow Mr Holland making his morning deliveries around the town. The Royal Mail, however, had stipulated that Mr Holland could not be filmed delivering the actual contents of his sack through the various letterboxes on his round. Now, a postman without letters, like a lumberjack without trees, cuts a sad figure on television, where pictures are rather important. As a result

the production team provided him with a supply of dummy letters which he proceeded to deliver, and which Liz, following behind out of shot and musing on her glamorous life as a TV researcher, was deputed to collect in a rubbish sack.

Although the television as confessional has been exploited widely today, back then, in Britain at least, it was a relatively new genre. Most people never expected to be interviewed on TV, and those whose stories were best suited to the medium were usually the very people who least sought the experience. Conversely those actively and over-enthusiastically putting themselves forward for broadcast usually turned out to have larger egos the less interesting their stories were, and were best avoided.

Good researchers such as Liz (and the dozens who have succeeded her) need to have well-developed antennae to spot the difference. They need to have a pretty hard head and a very warm heart: hard-headedness to seek out a good story and not to take no for an answer, and warm-heartedness to coax the best from often shy individuals who have no desire for the limelight. Researchers, then

as now, will often relate how a very powerful bond of trust and affection will build up between them and their interviewees. They come to the programme knowing that people are not props or puppets and that they need to be treated with sensitivity at all times – particularly when they are making themselves vulnerable and exploring the deepest recesses of their emotions.

But – and here that professional hard-headedness comes in again – a researcher has to learn who is able to deliver on camera and who is not. "Many a time in the early days people would open up to me only to clam up in front of a film crew," says Liz, who had to learn to read the temperaments of the many people she met. Often it was the youngsters who spoke with the least self-consciousness. In that first new-look programme from Rye, for example, a young lad called David, a singer in the local church choir, had impressed everyone with his heartfelt choice of hymn, "When Lamps are Lighted in the Town". David's father was a fisherman, and whenever he heard that hymn he would always think of his dad coming back home after a night's fishing. When the programme returned several years later David was still there and had become a fisherman himself.

Some years later the presenter Geoffrey Wheeler conducted a similarly simple but memorable interview, which he recalls with great fondness to this day. *Songs of Praise* was visiting the Rolls Royce engine plant in Derby and in the run up to the recording Geoffrey despaired of getting anything of interest. "We'd done an interview with the chap who'd supervised the technical side of the 1964 film *The Yellow Rolls Royce,*" he says. "But because he'd clearly done this sort of thing hundreds of times before, the interview came out as rather too practised and pat. Then I turned to another man twisting his cap in his hands and I thought "This is hopeless." I asked him if he was aware of God in his life and without a pause he said, 'Oh, yes.'"

Geoffrey was intrigued. The man told him that his job involved preparing a small but vital piece of aluminium without which the engines could not function. "I have a template," he explained, "and I draw around it, insert holes for the rivets, and then cut out the aluminium shape." "Oh," said Geoffrey, at a loss to see what this fascinating fact had to do with anything. "But don't you see?" the man replied. "My life is perfectly ordinary. Like a blank piece of aluminium. Then God lays his

template on my life and makes it very special." For Geoffrey it was the perfect sermon and a memorable moment to treasure.

The new-look programme was notable for another innovation: the choice of presenter. The programme has always alternated presenters, so this was no slight on Geoffrey's professionalism. It was just a matter of matching personality to programme style, and this first programme was intended to be more journalistic in feel.

Geoffrey was an avuncular charmer, not only a *Songs of Praise* fixture but also the amiable host of the long-running TV schools

quiz *Top of the Form.* In his place, for this first restyled edition, the producer and the editor wanted a news reporter. Step forward Michael Barratt, a seasoned print journalist and presenter of the early evening weekday current-affairs programme *Nationwide.* Although the programme's audience nearly doubled for this Rye edition, there was near mutiny among *Songs of Praise*'s regular fans, who wrote in to complain.

Michael Barratt's interview style was brisk and business-like. Committed to standards of journalistic objectivity, he refused to meet the interviewees

Michael Barratt

beforehand, encountering them for the first time on-screen. Geoffrey, by contrast, insisted on getting to know them first, establishing a rapport which he used as a springboard for his questions. Perhaps some of this showed on air; perhaps the viewers simply didn't like a change of presenter. Who knows? Either way, for many Michael was destined to play the role of Mr Grumpy to Geoffrey's Mr Nice.

The journalistic edge that Michael Barratt brought to the programme was important because it established *Songs of Praise* as a programme that could respond quickly to changing national events. People could no longer point at it and accuse it of being (if it ever had been in the first place) a cute travelogue focusing on the niceties of village life that had been miraculously preserved since the 1950s.

Indeed Roger Hutchings, who served as series editor between 1984 and 1993, has gone as far as to say that, from the late 1970s onward, the *Songs of Praise* editor needed to be tuned in to the news every hour, on the hour, so as to be able, if necessary, to react to current events as they were happening. Not that *Songs of Praise* ever considered itself a documentary news strand. It was a programme of congregational hymn-singing, at

Below: Former series editor Roger Hutchings.

bottom, infused with the spiritual reflections of ordinary men and women living in the real world. And that real world is not always neat, tidy, and pretty. There would be wars (in the Falklands and the Gulf); there would be shootings (Dunblane); there would be national disasters (Aberfan and Zeebrugge) and international disasters (the 2004 tsunami); there would be bombings (in Northern Ireland and Iraq); and there would, inevitably, be bereavement.

Over time the programmes have framed all of these events, not reporting in the hit-and-run style of hardened news crews, but spending time with a community and gently drawing out the human stories – yes, of pain and loss,

but also of great fortitude and humility. And along the way they have reflected the often unreported dimension of bad news stories: the hope, courage, faith, and humanity that inspire people to endure the most heartbreaking of sorrows and find the strength to carry on.

Thankfully such stories of disaster and tragedy were not routine, and there was space for whimsy. Take the item on the last horse-drawn refuse cart in England, for example, which Michael Barratt found himself reluctantly boarding in Ross-on-Wye in 1977. A metropolitan chap with the 1970s TV presenter's fondness for sharp suits, kipper ties, and, on this occasion, a natty sheepskin "car coat", he found himself balancing, Steptoe-like, alongside his interviewee as the dust-cart made its painfully slow promenade round the town's one-way system. At the moment he had to cue the hymn choice the interviewee fluffed his lines and the whole laborious sequence through the traffic had to be filmed again – and again, and again, and

Michael Barratt aboard the last horse-drawn refuse cart going round and round the Ross-on-Wye one-way system.

again. This was trying enough for everyone, but the last straw came when a shopkeeper emerged on the fifth take with the offer of a cream cake for all the hard work. By now, as if starring in a well-rehearsed comedy sketch, Michael took one bite of the cake and squirted the cream down his brand-new coat. Liz, today giggling like a schoolgirl at the slapstick, remembers only that he was furious and, doubtless, grumpier than usual.

But she also remembers more poignant moments, such as an interview Michael did with Mrs Jeanette Hemming in Hackney, east London, that same year. Mrs Hemming was ninety-eight years old, and chose as her hymn "Jerusalem the Golden". She was aware that she was nearing the end of her time on earth and chose it because it gave her comfort as she approached death. Sadly, shortly after the interview had been filmed, but before the programme had been broadcast, Mrs Hemming died. As the team was preparing to make the necessary changes, news came that the family wanted the programme to go out as planned. Proof, if it were needed, of the sensitivity with which *Songs of Praise* handles its guests and of the importance it can play in memorialising people's everyday lives.

"That's just what we were striving for," says Andrew Barr, the then series producer. "I wanted to bring the freshness of the singing

Roger Royle

Favourite hymns:
"Just as I Am", "Ye Choirs of New
Jerusalem".

"I found *Songs of Praise* absolutely fascinating in the way it got to the heart of a community and got people to explain what impact their faith had on their lives. It was simple, direct, and from the heart. I've always considered my media work as part of my ministry as a Christian priest and dealing with letters from *Songs of Praise* was part of my pastoral care. The other thing I loved about my time on the programme was that I was there at a highly experimental and innovative phase when we were doing live link-ups with Christian communities all over the world. Chris Mann was in charge and I always said I wasn't being produced, I was being Mann-handled. It was such an exciting time. For example, I remember presenting from the ruins of [the old] Coventry Cathedral and doing a link-up with Cliff Michelmore in Dresden. We sang hymns in English and German and I felt the whole event was a very powerful Christian witness."

Roger Royle aboard the Wesley Express.

into direct relationship with the people who had told their stories so that the audience could see that their lives, hard or easy, were shared by others. My vision was to make the experience enjoyable and to get to grips with a faith that wasn't mediated through clerics and hierarchies. We really did have a window on the world and the stars were the people. *Songs of Praise* is the people."

Despite these high-minded intentions, Liz remembers that the official church hierarchy gave the programme very little support in the early days. "For a time the Church of England thought *Songs of Praise* very vulgar," she recalls. Indeed the late Donald Coggan, archbishop of York at that time, went into print with the assertion that *Songs of Praise* producers were ignorant and "broadcasting for the benefit of the gormless masses". This prejudice was also encountered at a lower clerical level when Liz turned up at a church in Chester to mobilise support for a forthcoming programme, only to be faced by an unenthusiastic vicar opening the door to her with the words: "Oh, I thought you lot would be coming. We had *It's a Knockout* last week." Regularly attracting audiences of 7 or 8 million, *Songs of Praise* learned not to mind these odd bouts of clerical snootiness.

"I didn't want it to be a ghetto programme but something that would appeal to everyone."

Jim Murray, former producer

At about this time a talented documentary film-maker named Jim Murray joined the team and got himself noticed with a groundbreaking programme from Brixton in south London. Eschewing the more traditional instruments normally featured on *Songs of Praise*, he drafted in reggae bands, steel drums, and gospel singers. He drew memorably on the talents of all the local people – and, in particular, on the intuition of a shrewd and much-loved priest, Fr Michael Armitage. Knowing his congregation all too well, Fr Michael advised Jim that it would be unwise to rehearse and film the event over two nights. "If you do that," he warned with a twinkle, "they'll think it's all over after the rehearsal and they won't turn up the next night." Jim listened, rethought his schedule, and filmed the OB on the first night. Perhaps because of that nervous edge, the programme had a spontaneous and heartfelt quality that Jim remembers to this day.

In all this he was capably assisted by the talented Fr Michael, a musician himself, who, knowing well the strengths and weaknesses of his congregation, had an instinctive knack for mixing different talents and musical styles. Indeed Jim was so impressed by his clerical collaborator that he eventually brought Michael into

Cameras capture the choir of Portsmouth Cathedral in full flow for the Remembrance Day programme in 2003.

the team as the programme's music adviser.

The point for Jim was to get "the magic of what I'd seen in rehearsals down the wire to your television set". And for that, he believed, a music adviser was necessary. Jim was recognised as a hard taskmaster, but one who produced the goods and who set standards of professionalism that were usually appreciated by the churches and communities he featured. To this end he even produced an explanatory pamphlet outlining what he expected of

The cast of *The Goon Show* (l-r): Harry Secombe, Michael Bentine, Spike Milligan and Peter Sellers, 27 May 1951.

participants at rehearsals and recordings.

"They appreciated it," he says. "They wanted to be shown at their best and if the music personnel weren't there, they upped their game and looked into what resources they had further afield. I explained that this was national telly not amateur hour from the village hall and they responded to it. They knew we had to apply the same professional standards to this programme as we would to any other."

Given his temperament, therefore, Jim was perhaps not the obvious choice of director to work with children and animals, as he did in

1982 at a Palm Sunday programme from Wells Cathedral. Feeling that the programme would lack life if all the children were in neat rows, he had all the seating removed. At a signal from him the cathedral doors were pushed open and in the kids charged, thousands of them, led by a donkey. Great. But not quite good enough for Jim who, despite the logistical nightmare and the parental protests, got them to do it again – and, for good measure, a third time. They were still flooding in when the hymn had finished. No one could argue, however, that the end product did not look stunning – justifying the time, effort, and perhaps just a few tears.

The following year saw him flying out with a team to the Falklands, where *Songs of Praise* was the first non-news programme to film from the islands since the conflict had ended in June of 1982. Producer/ director David Kremer, who flew out with his colleague Wendy Dyer, remembers that "the welcome was total and the whole thing was a huge community event". They had flown out ten days before the OB, and David and Wendy researched both for the main programme and for the documentary that followed on the quiet heroism of the islanders under occupation. Since, theoretically, no women were allowed on the military plane, "W. Dyer" was assumed to be a man

Songs of Praise revisits the Falklands with Aled Jones and crew: Mike Jackson (camera); Susan Keirby (production coordinator); Adrian Tomlin (sound); Richard Carruthers (assistant producer).

Above: A view of Stanley and Christ Church Cathedral.

Below: Steeple Jason Island, the Falklands.

and the two were billeted together. With the mix-up apparent, David was smartly put up in the rector's spare room.

Once again, *Songs of Praise* was breaking new ground and extending the possibilities of what could be achieved within the framework of a hymn-singing programme. The lighting may have looked a little severe – it was provided by the military and consisted of landing lights that were not needed on the airstrip – but it only added to the atmosphere of adventure and celebration over 7,500 miles away from home.

Then the real hostilities broke out. Hostilities that, in popular television terms, put the Falklands in the shade. In 1983, conscious that the BBC was trouncing them in the Sunday early evening schedules, ITV decided to retaliate by launching its own hymn-singing programme, *Highway*, presented by the legendary *Goon Show* performer, comedian, and fine tenor, Harry Secombe. For a time he was up against his fellow thespian and comedian Thora Hird, whose summer series, *Praise Be!*, was a collection of lovingly compiled *Songs of Praise* highlights – and hugely popular in itself.

On air the competition was lighthearted. Whenever a helicopter flew over, interrupting a *Highway* recording, for example, Harry would quip that it was Thora hovering overhead and trying to disrupt things. In ITV and BBC executives' offices, however, the development was to be considered with the utmost seriousness. This

"The point was to make the show accessible so that you didn't have to belong to the club in order to watch and enjoy."

Stephen Whittle, former series producer

The first gospel music programme, Southwark Cathedral, London.

was ratings war, and pretty soon ITV was clearly winning, with a million or so more viewers every week. For a time the then head of BBC television religious programmes, Colin Morris, is said to have been working on a counter-attack: in the event of Thora's death (she was then seventy-two) he was considering as her replacement Diana Dors. In the event, the blonde bombshell was never dropped as, sadly, Ms Dors died at the young age of fifty-three, predeceasing Thora, who went on to live to ninety-one, and who established herself as an irreplaceable national treasure. But

Songs of Praise clearly had to up its game.

This it did with, among others, a groundbreaking event held at Southwark Cathedral – the first of many black gospel spectaculars broadcast since then. Producers

Chris Mann and Jim Murray had studied with some sadness accounts of the cool-to-hostile reception received by West Indian immigrants coming to Britain from the late 1940s onward. But what saddened Chris most, as a devout Christian himself, was that the churches were no more welcoming than anyone else. It was time to make amends.

"We packed all the gospel choirs in London into Southwark and frankly couldn't control the exuberance. No point saying, 'Hold it while we change cameras.' When the singing began it was like a nuclear bomb and we just filmed it. The singing was extraordinary, the pictures were extraordinary, and to this day I count it one of the highlights of my career."

By now you will have gathered that Chris Mann ("Mr Chris" as he was affectionately known in some quarters) is someone who thinks BIG. To him this *Songs of*

Diane Louise Jordan and crew in Lourdes.

Praise edition was nothing short of "a huge moment in history". It was certainly a landmark event in popular broadcasting: here was the BBC's religious department confidently and vibrantly presenting as mainstream what many had seen as minority worship on the fringes of the Christian landscape.

Another entry in a long list of "firsts" was a *Songs of Praise* from the French monastic and ecumenical community of Taizé. This, too, was outside the comfort zone of the programme's faithful, many of whom were mystified by the simple, repetitive chants and informal candlelit setting, and who wondered whether they had mistakenly pressed the wrong button on their television set. Many others, however, welcomed it as a window on another kind of singing and on another kind of spiritual experience.

In these reactions is encapsulated

Songs of Praise's abiding dilemma. Does it follow or does it lead? Does it abandon experiment and innovation and give its loyal audience what it has had Sunday after Sunday, or does it allow its creative and committed staff to take that same audience on a journey of musical discovery, leading them into new experiences that they will in time find as familiar as the old? This is a question the team has been wrestling with for fifty years and will doubtless continue to ponder for many more to come.

Another of the innovations that *Songs of Praise* pioneered was the link-up between countries and continents. The BBC's motto is "Nation shall speak peace unto nation." "Why," wondered Chris Mann, "can't it be 'Nation shall *sing* peace unto nation', and why can't we fill, say, Trafalgar Square at Christmas and put people in touch with Christians around the world?"

Left: Producer Chris Mann on his African travels.

Middle: Chris Mann takes a trip across the Zambian plains.

Bottom: Christmas hymn-singing from northern Kenya.

The answer, unsurprisingly, was money – or lack of it. So when Chris hit on the idea of a New Year's Eve live link-up to Kenya, to the village of Muchacos outside the capital, Nairobi, he was told immediately that it was a non-starter. In no way could the then head of TV religion, Stephen Whittle, give the go-ahead for an outside broadcast from Africa on the budget available. So "Mr Chris" worked on a plan B.

What about a live *audio* link-up on the night of recording in Trafalgar Square intercut, at the editing stage, with previously recorded *pictures* from the live event in Muchacos? Combine the two and, while you wouldn't have a live transmission, you would have a recorded programme of a live event in two continents with all the excitement that entailed.

The plan was nervously waved

through and Chris, without engineering or clerical back up, agreed to project manage the entire Africa operation on his own and fly out unaccompanied. It helped, of course, that he has a degree in electrical engineering – but he was still taking on a vast job. It helped also that Stephen Whittle, formerly a religious journalist in Geneva with the World Council of Churches, had extensive contacts within the African church – but it did not guarantee a programme. It was a journey without maps.

This was an era when satellite broadcasting was in its infancy and, even if available, would have been ruinously expensive. Chris was left, therefore, with no option but to invoke the season of goodwill,

Christmas carols in Trafalgar Square, London.

Kenyan men prepare to sing during the live link-up.

mention the BBC, and cadge the lines for free from BT. Once in Kenya he hired a Reuters film crew and a local secretary, bought speakers and an amplifier from a hi-fi store, and got a Nairobi Post Office engineer to run a cable to the village. As a result he now had, on-site, the makings of a rudimentary OB unit (made out of packing cases held together with string) and was in business.

Knowing which shots were to be filmed in Trafalgar Square Chris then plotted the shots of the Kenyan choir: groups of two facing to the left on the second two verses of the hymn to match groups of two facing to the right in London singing the first two verses. And so on. Keep up at the back. But although the *pictures* were being recorded, the *sound* of the African choir was being fed live to Trafalgar Square and vice versa. "I touched these two wires together,"

says Chris, "and suddenly the sound of the London choir boomed round the village. 'Hello, Muchacos!' came the presenter Roger Royle's voice from 4,000 miles away. 'Hello, London!' came the reply. The atmosphere was electric."

There is an interesting and, for Chris, quite fortunate postscript to the evening. Earlier he had asked some villagers to move the makeshift hut housing the electrical gear to another location because

it was spoiling a shot. To do so they used Chris's hired station wagon in which they discovered, in the back nestling behind the driver's seat, a black mamba. To this day Chris breaks out in a sweat at the thought of driving back to his hotel in the dark and finding himself entwined in the embrace of one of the most venomous snakes in the world. Happily he made it in one piece and could contemplate a job well done. Or, rather, half a job well done. For if the live event in front of a couple of hundred people in Africa and England had been a total success, the broadcast to an audience of 10 or 11 million was still to be made. And by a whisker it almost wasn't.

The next day, beaming with satisfaction, Chris drove to the airport with his unedited film (known in the trade as the "rushes"). These would then be cut into the London recordings to make the final programme. Before he set off for the airport he first had to stop off at the offices of the National

Council of Churches to hand over a cheque for the not inconsiderable help they had provided. To save time he had arranged for an official to be standing on the pavement outside but, when he arrived, there was no one. He was therefore forced to leave the car unattended, dash up five flights of steps and hand over the money in person.

"Thankfully I make it a golden rule never to be separated from my rushes," says Chris. "So I ran upstairs with my briefcase and a bag with all the film and returned to find... the car had been stolen." With only a couple of hours until the plane was due to leave, he was in a sweat. No plane meant no film. And no film, he reasoned, probably meant no job. The police were called and by some stroke of luck the car was found. He dashed to the airport only to see the jet taxiing away from the terminal. Nothing for it but to pull rank. Drawing himself up to his full and not inconsiderable height he raised the bag containing the rushes aloft and boomed to the

bewildered check-in staff, "This is an interview with your president. If it does not go out tonight on the BBC I want to know who is responsible." The plane returned to the terminal and Chris was put in club class and then handed a glass of champagne to steady his nerves. By such threads do *Songs of Praise* programmes hang.

The Kenya Christmas link-up ended a brilliant year for the programme and one which raised the bar another notch. It was a good way to ring out the old because, in ringing in the new, *Songs of Praise* was also welcoming in its twenty-fifth anniversary year. It was a quarter of a century old and still in business.

CHAPTER 3

1986–92: Consolidation and Expansion

From political controversy to the karaoke years

In many ways 1986 began like any other year, with the *Songs of Praise* team scanning the map of the British Isles and preparing its new year's run of shows. This year, however, was special. The programme was celebrating twenty-five years as "the nation's favourite" and, while it could look back with quiet satisfaction on its past, it also needed to safeguard its future. It was the ideal opportunity to take stock. Ever conscious that a long-running programme was in constant danger of becoming tired or formulaic the staff were determined to think up new ways of making it fresh and attractive. The old saying "If it ain't broke don't fix it"

doesn't always apply to the rapidly changing world of television. For one thing, technology is constantly evolving, providing producers (and their competitors) with new opportunities for innovation. And secondly, as these possibilities increase, so too do the audience's expectations. If *Songs of Praise* chose to rely on its enviable reputation and stand still, it would soon be overtaken by the competition. So the dilemma, as usual, came down to this: how do you move forward in a medium of constant change while at the same time taking with you the loyal

core audience that is content with the way things are?

Twenty-five years on, in *Songs of Praise*'s fiftieth anniversary year, the challenge still remains, with Tommy Nagra and his team constantly devising ways of future-proofing the show and continuing to ensure that it is relevant to the widest possible audience. The programme is being extended to other media such as the internet and the BBC iPlayer, and will be extended further, to media yet to be invented. An interactive *Songs of Praise* could split the screen

Aled Jones filming in Jerusalem,
2009.

"*Songs of Praise* is not just another show. It's a way for people
to get in touch with their spiritual nature. I'd be lying if I said
I used to watch it regularly as a kid. I was usually in the bath
listening to the Top 40. *Songs of Praise* makes you feel good.
It uplifts the soul. When everyone sings a hymn such as 'How
Great Thou Art' you cannot help but feel stirred. I think in a
way hymns are nothing to do with the church. They are the pop
songs of their time. I think when a good hymn comes together
there's nothing to beat it. *Songs of Praise* plays a massive role
in preserving these hymns and without it the newer hymns
wouldn't come through. Also, as a viewer, you know that every
shot will be perfect and that's because we spend four days
making half an hour. I'm also aware that we are getting into
the heart of a community and mixing with such interesting and
warm-hearted people. I love it."

into two, or three, or four, with
permutations of button-pressing
giving access to unbroadcast
material with selected interviewees.
The team might take their cue from
DVD producers and record "extra
features" to be viewed at leisure
after the programme proper has
been broadcast. It might assemble a
downloadable *Songs of Praise* hymn-
book to give viewers the option of
selecting their own choices from
a virtual archive of hymns ancient
and modern. It might… But we are
running ahead of ourselves.

In 1986 under the then series
producer, Stephen Whittle,
the process of reinvention was
already under way. He had begun
it four years earlier when he was
appointed. As the programme's
unique selling point was its
singing he realised that the musical
standards had to be of the highest.
As a result he decided that a
permanent full-time music adviser
was to be one of the programme's
prime requirements. The job went
to the church music specialist Bob
Prizeman, who was known to the
programme as the composer of the
Songs of Praise signature tune and
who was taken on to continue the
work begun by Michael Armitage.

"It truly is a public access
programme," says Bob. "You are
absolutely dealing with local
talent. When I joined, the singing
talent was there. It just needed

Below: Conductor Noel Tredinnick in rehearsal for the *Songs of Praise* 2003 Remembrance Day programme from Portsmouth Cathedral.

to be corralled." The problem he encountered was that sometimes the conductor or organist was not of the standard required for a Sunday evening broadcast on BBC One. Initially his job involved musical first aid, ensuring that the variable standards he encountered could be licked into some sort of unified shape. Before the main rehearsal singers can expect a couple of extra choir rehearsals. "If you knew there was a problem you had enough time to make a few calls," he says diplomatically, adding, "You'd never

fire anyone but there might be a bit of moving of microphones and personnel."

The question was: how good should the choral singing be? This has been a dilemma the programme has sought to resolve in different ways over the years. To what degree is it about a group of local people giving of its best in a natural and unadorned way, and to what degree is it responsible for broadcasting a semi-professional end product? *Songs of Praise* increasingly opted for more musical intervention

and brought in the services of a professional conductor to ensure the best standards of performance. Northern Ireland had used a conductor from quite early on, but it was under Bob that the decision was made to use one routinely.

Another addition (to save journeys between the control booth and the hall) was a telephone at the conductor's rostrum. This was connected to the OB van, or "scanner", as it is known, and enabled the music adviser to speak to the conductor quickly to discuss

Below: Conductor Noel Tredinnick in rehearsal for the *Songs of Praise* 2003 Remembrance Day programme from Portsmouth Cathedral.

Simply the best (1)

The former head of BBC religious broadcasting, Ernie Rea, remembers dropping in on a programme and going backstage to compliment the team on a brilliant show. "I went into the scanner after one particularly fine programme," he says, "and I saw David Kremer, the director, with his head in his hands.

"What's the matter?" I asked.

"I came in a bar early on the soprano," he said, and nothing I could say about the brilliance of the programme could console him.

In due course I heard the full story. The next day the soprano had phoned David to apologise for coming in a bar late."

how to improve the singing. Thanks to the positioning of the microphones and the sound balance in the scanner the effect heard by the conductor in the church or cathedral may not be that ultimately heard by the TV audience and, as a result, the music adviser, as final arbiter, needs to convey his impressions. This is where the phone came in. A "ring ring" would periodically interrupt proceedings front of house, prompting on-stage gurning by the choir and a conspiratorial sense of solidarity between conductor and singers as they were kept in line by the mystery caller (in fact, usually one Bob Prizeman).

With the congregation, of course, different standards would apply.

Conductor Noel Tredinnick communicating with the "scanner" in rehearsal for the Songs of Praise 2003 Remembrance Day programme from Portsmouth Cathedral.

In his day Andrew Barr preferred the spontaneous approach over endless retakes of a particular hymn. "Usually the first take was the best anyway," he says, "and by the time the director says 'Let's do it again' for the seventeenth time, the congregation is in a panic." Or worse. "I once found myself in Wakefield Cathedral under instructions to tell the choir to sing 'This Joyful Eastertide' again and again. By the sixth time I was ready to fall on my sword as the mood of joy had long since passed. By the seventh I thought I'd better leave town the next day, or preferably that evening, such was the sense of venom that was building up. That can be counter-productive. I think the only time I filmed the congregation twice was in Ross-on-Wye when a chap's tooth fell out on camera."

The early output in the twenty-fifth anniversary year was characteristically varied and included visits to a synagogue, three cathedrals, and a prison. But it was a broadcast from the Spalding Tulip Parade in 1986 in the Lincolnshire fenlands that was to stand out, for better or worse. The Spalding Tulip Parade is an unlikely setting for a political controversy, you would have thought, but political controversy was what it generated, provoking angry exchanges in the local press for weeks afterwards.

Beautiful though the fields of tulips are in springtime, there is only so much you can say about bulbs on prime-time television without the public's interest wandering just a little. Accordingly, the film featured people with other than horticultural stories to tell. One was Carol Burton, a Quaker woman whose Christian pacifism, CND membership, and opposition to a Royal Navy stand at the festival put several noses out of joint and prompted one ex-serviceman to complain about the BBC's infiltration by "political lefties".

The other interviewee, however, was much more involved with issues nearer home. She was Margaret Wheatley, a health visitor who had been filmed visiting a relatively deprived part of the town and talking to families who lived in poorly built houses with outside lavatories. She talked about the health problems many of these people faced as a result and mentioned briefly the rising unemployment the town's young men were experiencing as farms became increasingly mechanised. The simple point she was making was that she, as a Christian, felt the need to help people less fortunate than herself. This was far from being a political manifesto. But not everyone saw it that way.

Under the headline "Political *Songs of Praise*" the *Spalding Guardian* thundered magisterially that "among the flowers there was a worm in the bud" and proceeded to quote residents unhappy with the thrust of the programme. Lively correspondence ensued and the affair acquired all the trappings of a good local row. Some praised the programme for its honest look at social issues that many wished did not exist; some attacked it for unfairness and biased filming; and others merely wondered what all the fuss was about.

The response was instructive since, in miniature, the Spalding Tulip Parade got to the heart of the conundrum facing producers and editors week by week. While *Songs of Praise* is not a documentary strand, neither can it be a bland travelogue glossing over the realities of life. If, while tiptoeing through the tulips, local churchpeople felt that social issues needed to be raised, the programme

Spalding Tulip Parade with floats decorated with petals from local bulb production.

National Treasures (1) Dame Thora

"Thora was a great annoyance to me," says former *Songs of Praise* producer Roger Hutchings. What? How can he say such a thing about one of the programme's best-loved presenters of all time? Off with his head! Never fear, for this is meant as an expression of affection and admiration for the woman who first presented *Songs of Praise*'s companion programme *Praise Be!* in 1976 and who was, until her death in 2003 at the age of ninety-one, something akin to television royalty. "The really annoying thing," continues Roger, "was that you would spend huge

amounts of money making programmes which she then linked in her own show. And the end result was that she and her compilation programmes got a much bigger audience than our original broadcasts! But she was such a lovely lady that you couldn't hold a thing against her."

For Liz Barr, who worked with Thora for over twenty years, she represented a kind of innocence that we have now lost; she was part of a world where "neighbours were neighbourly and always helping one another out with small kindnesses". People related to her as a friend or as a member of the family and she, in turn, spoke to viewers as *her* friends (which they were), talking to them in her inimitable way as if they were in the room with her sharing a cup of tea. A woman of unshakeable Christian faith, she loved to say, in answer to the question, "When did you find God?", "I've never had to look. He's always been there."

had a duty to reflect that. But what of political balance? And how could *Songs of Praise* justify the inclusion of a CND voice in the programme? In keeping with BBC guidelines the producers do indeed strive for balance in all the programmes they make, but sometimes they achieve that balance over time. Yes, they could have invited a Royal Navy spokesperson to debate the issues of defence and deterrence with Mrs Burton but that, it was decided, would have made the programme more political, straying away from its hymn-singing brief. In the event the programme was able to argue that, over time, it had featured countless service personnel and ex-servicemen and women. It had broadcast memorable editions for Remembrance Day and had visited scores of army, navy, and air force bases around the country. Far from being partisan, the programme was, and still is, designed to reflect the many and varied faces of the population at large.

Later that year there followed memorable link-ups between Coventry and Dresden, and London and Tonga. The following year there were programmes from schools, shopping centres, and garrisons; programmes featuring jazz and gospel music and, of course, the traditional hymns beloved by so many. And then in 1988 there was the broadcast that has gone down in history as one of the most daring and technically challenging that had ever been undertaken: the 250th anniversary of John Wesley's spiritual epiphany, when he committed himself to popular evangelism and laid the foundations of what was to become Methodism.

In conjunction with the then British Rail's splendidly named "punctuality officer" and senior managers, it was arranged that three separate trains should be despatched from St Pancras, all loaded with combinations of singers, presenters, technical crew, and brass bands. The high point was to be when two of the trains met on a stretch of track where both tracks came together in parallel. To the accompaniment of song the two presenters, Sally Magnusson and Cliff Michelmore, greeted each other with a rousing "Ahoy, there!" and the rest has become broadcasting – and locomotive – history.

However, for every five bright ideas Chris Mann had before breakfast at least three or four were discarded before lunchtime – though the remainder became classics. Researcher Valetta

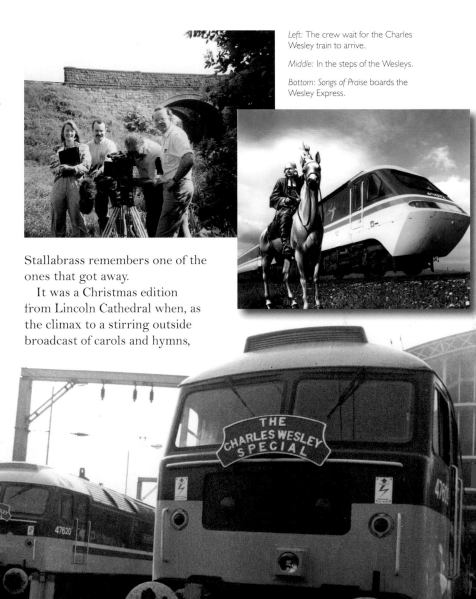

Left: The crew wait for the Charles Wesley train to arrive.

Middle: In the steps of the Wesleys.

Bottom: Songs of Praise boards the Wesley Express.

Stallabrass remembers one of the ones that got away.

It was a Christmas edition from Lincoln Cathedral when, as the climax to a stirring outside broadcast of carols and hymns,

*"Listening to people is
something I regard as
a huge privilege."*

David Kremer, producer

Top: Choirboys singing in the stalls.

Bottom: Lincoln Cathedral, Christmas 1984.

Chris (as only Chris could) got his secretary to dress up as an angel and climb onto the outside parapet of the west end, where she would be lit by spotlight as the programme closed. This would have been invention enough without Chris, by now gilding the lily, coming up with a finale to top even that. "Now, there's an airbase nearby, Valetta," he suggested helpfully. "See if you can arrange for the RAF to fly over Moscow dropping presents and get the Russian air force to fly

over Lincoln doing the same." He *was* serious. Valetta felt the need to check this out with Stephen Whittle and was given the simple instruction: "Forget it."

Valetta, though, remembers as a high point a more traditional programme – a Remembrance broadcast in 1988 from the Royal Hospital, Chelsea. For those worried by the programme's embrace of too much modernity, Remembrance editions have always provided a reassuring thread of continuity. This edition was no different, but it remoulded tradition for a contemporary audience and, not content with a static, chapel-bound treatment, it took some veterans back to the Somme and Ypres to film their reactions. Valetta remembers 96-year-old Frank Sumpter, in particular, seeing his brother's grave for the first time. These were men of the old school, who had been encouraged to keep their emotions to themselves. They were not given to self-pity or public displays of grief or sorrow. Encouraged by the sensitive but searching questions of the presenter, Cliff Michelmore, they now found themselves opening their hearts as never before and surprising even themselves by the pain they had kept within for so long. It is moments such as this that *Songs of Praise* has learned to

treasure, matching a mood to a hymn and thereby bringing both suffering and celebration to a profound and deeply moving point of resolution.

If, on the human front, *Songs of Praise* was constantly experimenting with ways of telling stories, on the technical front it was also exploiting the opportunities afforded by evolving technology. David Kremer, who has been described by one colleague as "someone who emerged from the cradle able to direct", took particular pride in a groundbreaking broadcast of the Festival of Nine Lessons and Carols from the chapel of King's College, Cambridge. The department had had the chapel in its sights for several years, but had been refused permission to film on the grounds that the cameras might be (and the lights certainly would be) too intrusive. The candle-lit atmosphere of the Christmas Eve service, so the opposition went, would be ruined if it were bathed in the glare of ghastly arc lamps. But this was to reckon without the new kit that the programme was enthusiastically pioneering.

There had been several nervous meetings with the King's College authorities before they eventually relented and, with latent misgivings, agreed to let the team in. Their gamble,

More than just a programme

There have been many times in *Songs of Praise*'s history when the stories of those featuring in the programme have resonated deep within the hearts of those making it. Presenter Pam Rhodes recalls interviewing Daphne Petersen from Falmouth, who had lost a daughter, two sons, and a granddaughter in a house fire. Although the pain was still raw and the grief still visible, she spoke honestly about the faith that had supported her through the most unimaginable loss. "I'm a mum," says Pam, "but could I have done that?" But then something beyond words took place and Daphne took Bethan, Pam's ten-week-old daughter, in her arms. What that "something" was, no one can tell, not even Pam. "But she hugged her," she says. "That was twenty-one years ago and Daphne hasn't stopped hugging Bethan since really. She's become an informal godmum."

Diane Louise Jordan

Favourite hymn:
"How Great Thou Art".

"*Songs of Praise* is like no other television programme I've worked on and I know it has a special place in the nation's heart. I think what makes it special is that the audience really believe (and I think they're right) that they own the programme. It's more than just a television experience because it really and truly interacts with people. Many people have told me that for them it really is a spiritual experience. Hearing stories of hope or of transformation is very uplifting, and if those stories have a resonance in your own life I honestly believe that can be quite healing. And there is something very powerful about a group of people coming together to share a musical experience. In fact sometimes when I am being filmed singing in the congregation I simply forget that we are making a television programme. I'm just caught up in the spirit-lifting, life-enhancing atmosphere of the whole event and I believe that my faith has grown more during the time I have been on the programme. Although they didn't realise it at the time so many of the people I interviewed were taking me further and further on my personal journey of faith."

however, was justified, and David remembers the evening as a total success. From the OB truck he realised that the programme was going well but he had these first impressions corroborated later. After the broadcast he was told by a colleague in the congregation that, as they waited for the service to begin, they were anxiously looking at their watches, wondering when the lights would come on. The first time they realised that the lights already *were* on was when a lone chorister broke the expectant silence with "Once in Royal David's City".

This experience merely reinforced David's conviction that the look of the programme mattered as much as the sound. It even mattered as much as the content. *Songs of Praise*'s strength has always been in its ability to assemble a team committed to all three. That commitment was expressed in blunter terms by a lighting director. "I can illuminate the place for you like a stadium," he once told David, "or I can light it. And lighting it will cost half as much again." The production managers first had to agree to this extra cost, of course, and, to their credit, David says, they did, realising that shooting the programme on the cheap was a false economy.

Some lighting directors, he also recalls, would approach their craft

King's College, Cambridge. It was from here that a groundbreaking broadcast of the Festival of Nine Carols came.

from the engineering point of view. The BBC then had precise technical specifications for the lights and the lighting tones, but shooting by the rule book, in David's eyes, often made people's faces look rather cold. "We sort of mocked this," he says, "and complained that faces on-screen were bathed in a *Songs of Praise* lilac." When he asked the lighting crew whether they could change the colour a little at the final edit he was told that, yes, technically they could but that they would need something in writing from the lighting director to allow them to do so. What had been recorded had been passed as correct according to the rules and altering it would be at the producer's personal risk.

By the late 1980s things were changing. As soon as newer, more flexible, lighting became available it was incorporated immediately, enhancing the programme greatly. The era of so-called "producer choice" in the early 1990s also gave producers more freedom to assemble exactly the crew

Coloured lighting is used to enhance a London
recording at St Bartholomew the Great's, with boys'
choir Libera.

"Its relevance earns it a place in the BBC One peak-time schedule."

Helen Alexander, former series editor

Below: Sally Magnusson on Bonfire Night.

they wanted and to use what David Kremer has described as "the artistic technicians" if they were thought better suited to a particular occasion.

Working with lights and microphones, however, is one thing. Working with people is quite another. The communities that appear in the final programme are, *de facto*, willing to collaborate with each other. They will have put any denominational differences behind them for the broadcast and will have agreed to work together in a spirit of friendship and shared enjoyment. Indeed the mere fact of collaboration will have caused many to question the need for such differences in the first place. But, although *Songs of Praise* tries (usually successfully) to foster such cooperation and interreligious harmony, it has, on occasions, admitted defeat. In 1984, for example, the Northern Ireland producer Ernie Rea, who was eventually to become the BBC head of religious broadcasting when the department moved to Manchester in 1992, produced a programme from the Protestant heartland of the Shankhill Road in Belfast. What was not widely known until the programme aired, however, was that there was a significant peace movement involving local Protestants and Catholics from the nearby Clonard Monastery off the

Falls Road. The programme had the makings of a classic – especially as it featured a local man, Jimmy Stewart, who had lost both legs as a result of an IRA bomb left in the Abercorn restaurant in the centre of town in 1972, and who had been filmed days earlier talking about the need for forgiveness and reconciliation.

The recording began and pretty soon Ernie realised all was not well. From the OB vehicle he saw that Jimmy was not singing. The next day he approached Ernie and told him he was not happy with

the presence of so many priests and nuns in the congregation and wanted to pull out. Ernie tried to persuade him to reconsider but he was adamant. The interview was pulled from the programme and all trace of Jimmy in the church was edited out. "Yes, he was an evangelical Protestant and he may have been uneasy with the priests and nuns but I believe to this day," says Ernie, with evident sadness, "that Jimmy had been got at by members of his community." It was an opportunity missed, for in Northern Ireland, even when

Below: Mortars for the finale of the programme from Lewes, 1989.

the Troubles were at their height, *Songs of Praise* was one of the few public platforms where people from opposite sides could come together comfortably.

Such tensions could exist on the mainland, too.

In 1989 the programme headed for the Sussex town

of Lewes, famed for its Bonfire Night celebrations. Memories in that part of the world are long and a strong anti-papist theme runs through the whole event as the town commemorates Protestant martyrs who were burnt at the stake during the persecutions of Henry VIII's daughter Queen Mary. It was felt that, though pretty, bonfires had a subtext of cruelty and oppression. In the past

they had roasted human flesh – ostensibly in the name of God – so they needed a fresh interpretation.

Now, if *Songs of Praise* had barged in and mounted its own bonfire event, this would have been an artificial imposition. If, on the other hand, it put an idea to the local council of churches and they liked it, they could run with it. In the event the churches loved the idea and backed the programme team to the hilt. The theme was to be "a festival of light", bringing together Christians in unity, fraternity, and reconciliation.

There was, however, intense opposition from the town's Bonfire Society, whose participation the programme had also hoped to secure – in vain. They declared that they wanted no part of the procession and that the programme was not welcome in Lewes. It is characteristic of the programme that it took soundings from the various churches in the area before deciding whether to press ahead or not. Only if there was a critical mass of local support could the programme

take place – which it did, with a spectacular firework display framing a full-throated rendition of "Joy to the World".

With Stephen Whittle now overall head of BBC TV religion, the new *Songs of Praise* editor was Roger Hutchings, a Methodist minister and a great grizzly bear of a man with a cascade of white hair and a ready line in irony and self-deprecation. Famed, for the moment, as the man who put a cap on Chris Mann's firework budget, he was shortly to oversee the programme at one of the most sensitive moments in its, and the nation's, recent history.

"There was some build-up to the first Gulf War and, though we knew it was going to happen [the allied aerial bombardment of Kuwait on 17 January 1991], we didn't know when," he recalls. "In the event it was a Thursday and I pulled out the tape of the programme due to go out that Sunday and saw that it came from Merthyr Tydfil. Now, I've no objection to Merthyr Tydfil, nor do I mind, in principle, doing a programme featuring a washing-machine factory, but that particular programme didn't somehow seem appropriate to the occasion."

It was time to pull strings and call in favours – at the double. Westminster Abbey was the first port of call, with a request for permission to mount a live programme that Sunday. It helped that, in contrast to the official church disapproval of thirty years before, the hierarchy was now well disposed toward *Songs of Praise*. It helped, too, that the then dean, Michael Maine, was an ex-BBC radio producer. Could Michael help?, Roger wondered. And how long would it take to get an answer? Within about twenty-five minutes of taking the original call, the dean was back on the phone with a yes.

Rigging Westminster Abbey is a big and expensive job. By the afternoon the engineering managers and OB department had been told that the programme had the go-ahead and they got down to erecting full lighting rigs for the nave and background lighting at the east end. Scaffolding was trundled in, cables were laid, and the scanner positioned – all in between the abbey's regular services.

To avoid any sense of Christian triumphalism the programme invited the Reform rabbi, the late Hugo Gryn, and the Islamic scholar, the late Zaki Badawi, to take part. As a former president of the Methodist Conference, and a public speaker of great presence and power, Colin Morris was chosen to present. He did so in a way that kept a packed abbey (and an audience of 10 million viewers) completely focused and engaged.

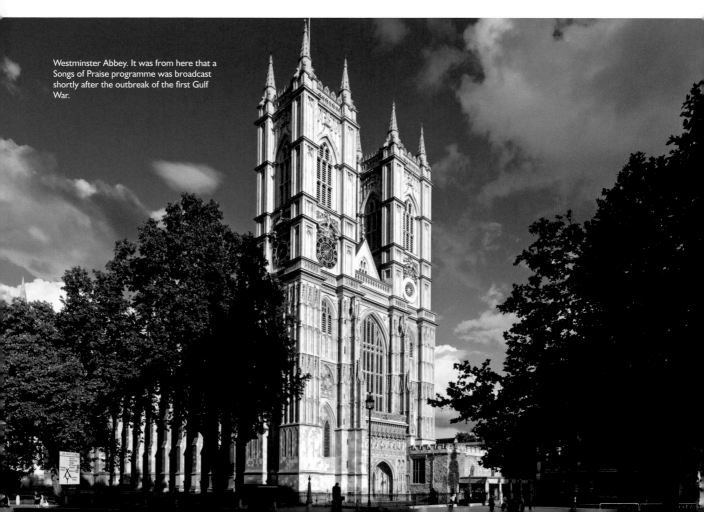

Westminster Abbey. It was from here that a Songs of Praise programme was broadcast shortly after the outbreak of the first Gulf War.

Pam Rhodes meets a member of the congregation at Liverpool Cathedral.

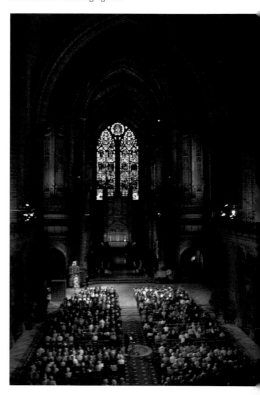

At Liverpool Cathedral, a camera in the aisle picks out faces from the congregation.

The following week, with more time to prepare, Colin and Pam Rhodes headed for Liverpool Metropolitan Cathedral, where Pam spoke to the families of service personnel. Then in the third and final of the live Gulf programmes, Dunblane Cathedral was chosen to reflect another aspect of this multi-dimensional conflict – the significant anti-war sentiment that had been strong in many parts of the UK, particularly in Scotland. This was not done uncritically. *Songs of Praise* has never been a mouthpiece or a platform for interest groups of any type, as those who observed Colin's tough line of questioning could attest that evening. But whatever views the British public held, 13 million of them tuned in to watch. A hymn-singing programme that could attract around a fifth of the UK population had, by any standards, to be taken seriously. Or so one might have thought.

In fact Stephen Whittle and Roger were about to embark on a campaign to prevent the programme being shunted to a much earlier time, 4.30 in the afternoon, with all the loss of profile that would entail. The then controller of BBC One, Jonathan Powell, argued that the programme's predominantly older audience (fifty-five plus) would be just as likely to watch at that time as at 6.40 p.m. Roger wasn't so sure and felt, on balance, that they wouldn't. As an audience of 6 million, say, slipped to 4 million, the next thing the controller would do, he reasoned, was argue the case for cutting budgets. As the budgets declined, the number of repeats would increase and the quality of the overall strand risked being compromised. This, in turn, would drive audiences away and justify a further cut. And so on, and so on, until there was nothing left.

Stephen and Roger held their ground and dug in for a fight. "It involved the director general, Michael Checkland, who was a Christian, and the chairman of the governors, Marmaduke Hussey, whose wife was a lady-in-waiting to the Queen," Roger remembers, before adding gnomically, "Now, whether those connections were made I have no idea and I wouldn't wish to say. But we fairly shamelessly tried to ensure that anyone who could influence the decision did." *Songs of Praise* kept its slot.

With one battle won, another was looming – this time on the domestic front, dividing the staff down the middle. The issue was whether to put the words to the hymns up on the screen. For detractors this brought to mind bouncing red dots and sing-along lyrics reminiscent of an East End knees-up. "Karaoke!" they screamed scornfully. They had a point. Why bother going to all the trouble of lighting an interior, filming it beautifully, framing faces, composing landscapes and cutting lovingly from tableau to tableau

A recording with popular boys' choir Libera.

when all people would now be looking at was the words?

On the other hand there was, in Roger's phrase, "a continuous dribble" of letters from viewers requesting that words be put on-screen. Torn between the audience and the team Roger decided that the only fair way to settle the matter was through independent objective research. "I spent proper money on this, taking proper audience soundings," he says. "And when the results came back they said that 70 per cent wanted words, 15 per cent thought it wasn't such a bad idea, and only the remainder was against. So, against the howls of my team, I said yes. If the audience says that's what it wants, then why not do it?"

The new look was inaugurated officially on 2 February 1992, when "Words Sunday" came from the town of Olney in Buckinghamshire (a town long associated with the hymn-writing tradition) and set *Songs of Praise* on course for the next phase of its evolution.

Atmospheric lighting enhances the beauty of Brecon Cathedral during a 2004 recording.

1993–2000: Thinking Big

The Giant's Causeway, Country Antrim. A *Songs of Praise* programme filmed here was one of the first to be broadcast after the team moved northwards.

How *Songs of Praise* entered the record books

The early 1990s was a time of great upheaval for the BBC religious broadcasting department. It moved north from London to Manchester taking, of course, *Songs of Praise* with it. At the time Stephen Whittle, who was opposed to the move, remembers renewed arguments over the timing of the programme, with pressure exerted once again to place it earlier in the afternoon.

Stephen successfully argued the case for leaving it where it was, on the grounds that to shift the department *and* the slot was effectively a vote of no confidence which risked demoralising an already unsettled staff.

Once relocated to Manchester the team carried on with business as usual, producing programmes from locations as various as the Giant's Causeway, the Blackpool illuminations, and "Constable country". In 1994 they logged another of many "firsts" when *Songs*

of Praise was broadcast live from the entrance to the Channel Tunnel. Presenter Alan Titchmarsh was on hand to welcome the first trainload of passengers, a group of Christians from northern France who joined in the singing with their English counterparts and did their bit for the *entente cordiale*.

Although this project tested the team's technical expertise to the full, it was as nothing compared to the challenge they set themselves later that year: to film, over a twenty-four-hour period, the passage of the sun across the heavens. The Global March for Jesus was the result, a programme of films recorded across the world as millions of people took to the streets in celebration and song. The idea had been suggested by the hymn-composer Graham Kendrick, and brought people from all over the world together to sing hymns. With his typical capacity for understatement, Chris Mann remembers that "more people than have ever been mobilised anywhere in the history of the species walked that day". And *Songs of Praise* viewers saw it first.

What was significant, technical wizardry aside, was that the programme harnessed the professional reporting skills of battle-hardened television news correspondents such as Kate Adie, Mike Wooldridge, and Philip Short, who lent the all-important

Right: Pam Rhodes with Chris Patten, governor of Hong Kong, in June 1997.

Below: The Global March programme made excellent use of the journalistic skills of the likes of Mike Woolridge, Kate Adie, and Philip Short.

Bottom left: Presenter Henry Sandon with singer Graham Kendrick.

journalistic edge that had made the programme so successful for so long. The nation's particular favourite, Pam Rhodes, had herself been a television news producer and reporter before she was headhunted to present *Songs of Praise*. She

believes that the programme's journalistic detachment lends it a particular strength. "I've interviewed people on death row," she says, "people who have lost family in shootings, in natural disasters, or on one occasion even through flesh-eating bacteria. We have filmed in Australia for the Olympics, in Hong Kong for the handover [to China], in Johannesburg for the release of Nelson Mandela. All big news events which we have tried to cover in a different, more positive way."

National Treasure (2) Sir Harry

"I was terrified when I was given the job of producing Harry's first *Songs of Praise* in 1995," Medwyn Hughes remembers. He need not have worried. Putting Medwyn immediately at ease Harry said simply, "You tell me what to do and I'll do it." The warm, funny, generous man people saw on-screen was the warm-hearted man they would meet in real life. What you saw was what you got, as everyone agreed. In one memorable programme he visited Holmfirth, setting for the BBC comedy series *Last of the Summer Wine*, to explore the whole experience of ageing. Whether talking to showbiz friends such as Thora, and Bill Owen and Kathy Staff (Compo and Nora Batty respectively) or to ordinary residents of this quiet Yorkshire town, his naturalness and gentle sense of fun shone through. These were qualities he retained even when cancer had been diagnosed and when, in 1998, he stepped down from the show. In a special Valentine's Day edition of the programme he and his beloved wife, Myra, renewed their marriage vows and Harry paid tribute to the *Songs of Praise* audience, who had given him strength during difficult times. Appropriately, perhaps, it was his turn to be interviewed, and he was able to explain how he, too, like countless people whose stories he had gently prompted over the years, had come to experience deep peace in the very midst of suffering.

Although presenters and researchers approach an interview with great sensitivity, the best of them also have an element of journalistic detachment to take their interviewees that little bit deeper into themselves until a human truth emerges which can instruct, ennoble, or humble us all. But those same researchers and presenters are merely temporary guests in a community and, as is the way with these things, must usually say goodbye sooner rather than later. In the course of the programme, friendships will certainly be made (and many will endure), but the journalist's privilege is the licence to enquire and then to move on.

In some cases this can be hard. Valetta Stallabrass, who left when the department moved to Manchester, felt guilty on occasions for having opened up a raw wound

Harry Secombe puts a ring onto Myra's finger as they renew their wedding vows.

only to have to walk out of a person's life altogether. One incident involved a woman who had lost her daughter in tragic circumstances and who was convinced she was being punished by God for something she had done in the past. At one point in the conversation her husband came into the room to join in and it was clear that he had no idea of what his wife was going through. It may have been a very healing moment for the couple (Valetta to this day believes it was), but she found it best not to recommend that the woman be interviewed on camera because it was all too raw and unresolved. "I've often thought about that and about other emotional conversations I've had," says Valetta, "and I think they're all part of the reason I went on to become a Samaritan after leaving *Songs of Praise*."

It is true that people are the raw material of *Songs of Praise*, but Valetta's experience proves that they are not manipulated as they can be on many TV talent or "reality" shows. Music adviser Bob Prizeman sums up *Songs of Praise* as "honest to humanity". The people we see weekly on-screen do not want to be stars. They have no ambition to get to the final, come out on top, secure the recording contract, or achieve fame and fortune. No, as participants in a true reality show they are just content to celebrate their faith and sing "songs of praise". And they are

Pam at Manchester United's Old Trafford, wearing a personalised football shirt.

out there in huge numbers, as the programme was to discover in 1995.

It all began on a train, with the producer John Forrest outlining his first thoughts on broadcasting a programme from the premier football league's "theatre of dreams", Old Trafford, home of the superteam Manchester United. "If we can fill this corner of the stadium," he explained, gesturing to a rudimentary diagram he had

drawn on a napkin, "we will have the largest *Songs of Praise* audience ever." He estimated it at around 7,000.

How did he know this? Well, John had attended a memorial service for the Manchester United manager, the late Sir Matt Busby. Seeing 7,000 people gathered for such a solemn but ultimately uplifting event convinced him that there was a huge pool of ordinary people – almost certainly not regular church-goers – who were attracted to this kind of public and communal celebration of life, possibly for reasons they could not entirely put their finger on. Could *Songs of Praise* perhaps use the same venue for a celebration of faith and thereby attract those people who had lost all contact with formal church-going? They could indeed.

Within two months of circulating plans of their intentions they had

filled the ground to capacity and had an overspill of eager volunteers waiting to take part. On the afternoon of the recording no fewer than 40,000 people filled the stands and sang at full volume. Present were bishops of the Anglican Church; committed Christians from communities, churches, and fellowships far and wide; and a mass of non-attenders who had either given up on church years ago or never even felt the need to step inside.

For the series editor at the time, Helen Alexander, this was a revelation. If there were any reservations among London executives about the programme's

The success of the programme aired from Old Trafford was later repeated when *Songs of Paise* was broadcast from Everton's Goodison Park, under the title "Merseyside Glory".

Cameraman Tom Ritchie and friend.

ability to be innovative and pull in a mass popular audience, this surely would quell them. "We were doing really well," says Helen, "and more than holding our own. But we were always looking to push back the envelope and with Old Trafford and others like it we did."

The first programme under her editorship had been a broadcast from the Meadowhall Shopping Centre in Sheffield, deliberately chosen as part of a new policy of "sanctifying secular spaces" – going outside the familiar church settings into places not associated with hymn-singing to do something unique, unusual, and surprising. What Helen needed, more than ever in the programme's history, was something that would stand firm against the competition. With *Highway* now gone, ITV was scheduling aggressively against the BBC, wheeling out its stars and celebrities, and devising a range of popular quiz and game shows for the tea-time audience.

"There was immense pressure on the BBC to follow suit," Helen remembers. "The spotlight was really on *Songs of Praise*. If the numbers now dropped critics could claim that the programme had been bringing in huge audiences only because there had been no competition. People were sure that, with a popular (secular) entertainment programme scheduled against us, viewers would watch that. But they didn't." All of which confirmed her in her belief that there was a place for a popular religious programme at peak time.

John Forrest's moment had arrived. Here was a producer, a devout Christian and popular innovator, who was absolutely committed to the twinning of entertainment and faith. His theological rationale was that everything in creation has a legitimate place in the worship of God. People can do it through

> *"I made no apology for bringing entertainment into the religious sphere. We worship God in many different ways and popular entertainment is one of them."*

John Forrest, former producer

poetry, art, and music – and through popular entertainment. "There is a place for high culture," he says, "and there is a place for popular culture which is loved and adored by people in their millions. The role of faith in that context has not been fully appreciated."

Here was a man to put this right. To some raised eyebrows he produced *Songs of Praise on Ice, Songs of Praise at the Panto, Songs of Praise at the Cinema* ("terrible acoustics but very comfortable seats"), *Songs of Praise at Disneyworld*, and a reprise of his Old Trafford success at Everton Football Club under the title "Mersey Glory". The audiences loved it. "They were great events attended by up to 40,000 people singing their hearts out," he remembers. "There were brass bands

Eamonn Holmes

Favourite hymns: "Jerusalem",
"Be Thou My Vision".

"*Songs of Praise* has a special place in my affections, as it was the first television programme I appeared on. I was twelve years old, a member of St Malachi's college choir singing with the congregation of the YMCA in Belfast, and I spent the entire broadcast looking at the camera. Then it was just such a privilege later to present the programme myself. There are very few programmes that can cement what is quite often a secular and fragmented society. And that is especially important in Northern Ireland. It is a big thing when *Songs of Praise* comes to town because it's a way of proving in a very concrete way that there are more things uniting people than dividing them. It's a tremendous healing thing and above all people want to be involved. This is a programme that cements different cultures, different religions, different age groups, and different peoples across the world. And it is incredible how it reaches out. Even if you're only an occasional worshipper, a lot of these songs reach out to our childhood. I love it."

and hymns, bishops, priests, and ministers, there were committed Christians and people who never went to church from one week to the next." It was community theatre, people's opera, and faith in song all rolled into one massively popular prime-time television programme that was daring to be different.

For if *Songs of Praise* stood still and refused to change it was doomed. When ordinary members of the public approached producers at outside broadcasts complaining that *Songs of Praise* wasn't what it was, they had to be gently told that, if it had remained what it was, it would not be on the air today. True, the loyal audiences did not always appreciate the black arts of TV scheduling policy. But producers and editors did – and had to take note of them in order to survive. Which was not to say that traditional hymns in traditional settings had had their day. There would always be a place for these but, from time to time, they might have to make way for newer forms of Christian expression from an emerging generation.

Hugh Faupel, later to succeed Helen as editor, devised a working motto: "Don't upset the same people two weeks running." As Hugh has never once even dreamt of upsetting his audience, the phrase needs some elaboration. What he was implying is that, while changes have to be made for the programme to survive, it is important not to alienate a loyal core audience which is sometimes slower to appreciate the need for such change. We are all of us most comfortable with the familiar, and both Hugh and Helen knew that, on balance, familiarity was what the established *Songs of Praise* audience tuned in to experience. But, equally, they reasoned that if there was sufficiently familiar fare on the menu one week, then the introduction of

Crowds gather at the shrine at Lourdes.

something new the next would not ruin their appetite. Who knows, they might even come to like it in time and ask for more. Nobody in his or her right mind tinkers with a much-loved format just for the sake of it. However, the guardians of that format have to balance innovation with preservation, making professional judgments and taking professional risks all the time. It is a high-wire act with no safety net.

One programme requiring such sensitive judgment was a memorable broadcast from Lourdes, the Catholic shrine in south-west France. Di Reid, who produced it, had a number of reasons for suggesting the location. The first was that, as a Catholic herself, she felt Catholic spirituality and some less familiar Catholic hymns were under-represented on *Songs of Praise*. The second was that she had discovered an exciting and visually arresting event would be taking place there under the auspices of the Handicapped Children's Pilgrimage Trust, which exists to take children with various levels of disability on pilgrimages to religious sites.

She did her research and concluded that the music and worship were extraordinary and unique. "It wasn't of professional quality but it was genuine," she remembers. "And the children were completely involved." Then she had to sell the idea to her boss, Helen

"The one thing I learned was the power and the depth of the faith of ordinary people."

**Di Reid,
former producer**

Alexander. "I explained that there were children with disabilities who couldn't really sing. But I also said that if what she wanted was people praising God then she wouldn't see better. Peak-time television? Children? Tambourines? Helen swallowed hard and OKed it." She would not be disappointed.

Di realised that she needed specialist musical assistance, so they brought in the services of a drummer, a keyboard player, and a church conductor who worked with the children and their carers to shape the raw material, highlighting their abilities and bringing out the best in their performance. "If you do this kind of thing well," says Di, "you don't impose, you enable." The next thing to do was get a presenter on board. Who better for a children's event than *Blue Peter*'s own Diane Louise Jordan? It was to be her first programme of many and made a lasting impression on her.

Beyond the Lourdes grotto and chapel, however, the souvenir shops made a lasting impression on Ernie Rea, then head of religious broadcasting, who had gone along to offer encouragement and support in the event of logistical difficulties. An Ulster Presbyterian minister who had spent part of his ministry on the Shankhill Road in Belfast, he would not perhaps have selected Lourdes as a destination

of first choice anyway. But if the shops selling such memorabilia as the Blessed Virgin Mary ashtray and the St Bernadette flick-knife confirmed his worst suspicions, the recording and the subsequent broadcast dispelled them. "I changed my attitude to Lourdes completely," he says. "I had my reservations about the dangers of exploiting vulnerable people and of raising their hopes but I was won over totally. I saw one young lad of about twelve with cerebral palsy and he was shaking uncontrollably during the mass. Then a young priest came up to him and gave him a hug and he took the wafer without shaking at all. Now, that boy may have gone home with the same condition but he will also

have gone home knowing that he was completely loved. It was a revelation to me."

There was, however, the small matter of the tambourines. As Di was soon to discover, one of the characteristics of the tambourine is that it gets everywhere and makes the post-production music mix a nightmare. You want to raise a vocal, you can't unless you take the tambourine with it; you want to accentuate a flute, you can't unless you accentuate the tambourine as well. Just as a mass was about to be recorded with the professional musicians and the children, a helpful steward appeared and distributed… tambourines… to the delight (naturally) of the singers. "You told me there'd be no tambourines!" came an exasperated wail from the sound supervisor. Too late. Too late.

"Inspirational music is part of people's lives."

Hugh Faupel, former editor

In the event the broadcast was not only a musical success but a success, too, in terms of its understated theological intentions. The programme looked at the issue of disability and at the difference between healing and cure. It also looked, by implication, at how disabled people are conventionally treated in churches. It did so not heavy-handedly but in an accessible and deeply human way. There was one girl called Emma, for example, who had Down's syndrome and was filmed taking her first communion. After the broadcast a number of vicars and ministers wrote in to say how they had been forced to rethink their previous convictions about the appropriateness of giving communion to a person with learning difficulties. "We raised these things in a sort of blink-and-you'll-miss-it way," says Di. "But perhaps that's enough to plant a seed."

The perennial *Songs of Praise* dilemma raised by the Lourdes programme – how far to lead its audience and how far to follow – was encapsulated in the following year when an event of unprecedented emotional magnitude took the whole country by surprise and left *Songs of Praise* rewriting the rule-book. The death of Diana, Princess of Wales, put the nation into shock – and the production team into overdrive.

The next Harry Secombe?

In the late 1990s *Songs of Praise* producer Medwyn Hughes was invited out to lunch by the then BBC head of religious broadcasting, Ernie Rea. The hugely popular and much loved Harry Secombe had been lured back to the BBC some years earlier after a decade as the face of ITV's *Highway*, and was now keeping the programme high in the ratings. His future was assured but Ernie casually wondered whether there was anyone out there among the younger generation who had comparable singing potential to present the show. "Who's the next Harry Secombe?" he asked.

A couple of suggestions were exchanged, then Medwyn ventured his fellow Welshman Aled Jones. Aled had established himself as a child singing sensation with the unforgettable "Walking in the Air" but, after his voice had broken, he'd slipped from the public eye, studied music at the Royal Academy, and trained as an actor.

"Hmm," said Ernie, recognising a good idea when he heard one, and the lunch resumed. Aled presented his first programme in 2001 from Bangor Cathedral, where he had been a chorister. The rest, as they say, is history.

"I was telephoned at around 7 a.m. with the news," says Helen, who was attending a conference in Geneva at the time. "The first thought I had in my half-awake state was, 'Thank heavens it's Monday.'" Even allowing for the time difference, however, it wasn't. It was well and truly Sunday morning, and she decided that a special programme – live, of course, and from a standing start

– had to go out in just under twelve hours. The director Steve Benson flew from Manchester to London along with David Kremer, who had organised an OB crew. Steve arrived on the steps of St Paul's as the scanner and five cameras pulled up. Pam Rhodes was summoned from Suffolk. And, soon after, Helen's plane touched down at Heathrow.

"When people criticise *Songs of Praise* they often say it's people in a holy huddle out of touch with the real world," says Helen. "They're wrong, of course, but they could have seen that for themselves that Sunday afternoon and evening." Amid the wall-to-wall news coverage that day a short announcement had been made that a special service was to be broadcast live from St Paul's in the *Songs of Praise* slot. From nowhere crowds began to arrive, queueing around the cathedral in unprecedented numbers and ensuring that even the service itself made news.

Inside the cathedral the live OB crew was doing what it always did in similar circumstances (if there *had* ever been similar circumstances). Lights were being hung, cameras were being positioned, and Steve was planning his shooting script. The hymns were being chosen and the choir was being rehearsed. Even the staff of St Paul's, from distinguished clerics to obscure vergers, commented enviously on the team's swift response to events and said how much they had learned pastorally from the experience. Such is the standing of the department at events such as this – and word has always travelled on the OB grapevine that *Songs of Praise* is a consummately professional outfit – that, unusually, BBC television news agreed to a live feed of pictures of the aircraft returning Diana's body. Steve split the screen and, to the perfect accompaniment of a sung psalm, allowed the outer reality to mingle

Floral tributes swamp Kensington Palace gardens and bear witness to the public grief that *Songs of Praise* was able to play a unique part in expressing and comforting.

with the shared inner experience, producing a near-sublime broadcasting moment. Could anyone doubt this was public service broadcasting at its best?

So, was the programme leading or following? By some mysterious alchemy it was doing both. It was reflecting the growing mood of the country but also, in forty minutes of commemoration, giving a shape to that mood when people were too shocked even to make sense of their own feelings. Of course there would be more outpourings of grief in the days and months to come – and of course the world's media would be there to track them. But *Songs of Praise* was the first single broadcast to take the shards of those raw, unresolved emotions and craft them into an event that gave the nation a common platform for its grief and provided the kind of solace that many ordinary men and women photographed in the streets were literally crying out for.

St Paul's Cathedral. It was from here that a live broadcast came following the death of Diana, Princess of Wales in 1997.

CHAPTER 5

2000 Onwards: The Millennium and Beyond

Life begins at fifty

The Diana programme had set a benchmark for what *Songs of Praise* could achieve when marking moments of grief and national tragedy. What was needed now was a comparable spectacular full of joy and celebration. Taking over the reins of the programme in 1998, Hugh Faupel decided that the obvious moment to make a big splash was the upcoming millennium celebration. The team set to work almost immediately.

The result was a huge success. Three programmes beforehand built up the expectation and prepared the audience for a live broadcast on the first Sunday of the year 2000, bringing over twelve months of preparation to a stunning climax. The Millennium Stadium in Cardiff was packed

Pam Rhodes appears on a giant TV screen above the audience at the Millennium Stadium, Cardiff.

The event was attended by His Royal Highness the Prince of Wales and the young princes, William and Harry.

Pam Rhodes and Don Maclean guide children through rehearsal in the empty stadium.

with 70,000 people in full voice. The guest of honour, the Prince of Wales, brought his sons along; Bryn Terfel and Cliff Richard performed to the accompaniment of massed bands and an orchestra of a hundred harps, and a packed stadium sang in a very special New Year. It was, Hugh remembers, "astronomically big", and made the front pages of the national newspapers. It was also, given the exchange rate at the time, the first $1 million programme in the history of the entire series. Now, in case anyone should think this was a flagrant self-indulgence and a waste of the licence payers' hard-earned cash, it needs to be stressed – as Hugh is keen to do – that the money technically paid for at least four other programmes, thereby squeezing the maximum amount of celebration, inspiration, and unabashed entertainment from this once-in-a-lifetime event. True to form *Songs of Praise* was clocking up another first.

No sooner was the millennium over than Hugh started planning for the next major milestone: the fortieth anniversary of the programme. For this he wanted a big musical event held, not in a cathedral, but in an iconic venue known the world over for its association with song.

Pilgrim through this barren land

Alan Titchmarsh

Favourite hymn:
"Here I Am, Lord".

"I always try to put myself in the role of Everyman, not that of a Bible-basher. I have the immense privilege of talking to people who have often been through tough times and run the gamut of human emotions. I'm just helping them to get across what faith means to them and, I hope, to convey the amazing sense of the power of goodness. It is incredibly uplifting to be in a packed church as part of a living community singing its heart out. Whatever your mood you always feel better at the end of it than you did at the beginning. I feel very strongly that *Songs of Praise* is part of Sunday evening. In its quiet way it reflects qualities of stoicism and the stiff upper lip. I have interviewed people with harrowing stories to tell, but I have always been hugely impressed and humbled by their resilience in times of crisis. More than anything the programme reflects that and proves to the world how ordinary people continue to use faith as the bedrock of their existence."

It had to be the Royal Albert Hall. Ticketed at a nominal price, it was an immediate sell-out. The idea, simplicity itself, could not have been truer to the original intention of the programme four decades earlier – to fill the space with singers singing songs of praise. So successful was this mass sing-along that the decision was made for it to become a regular feature in the programme calendar. The seed was sown for what would later turn into the *Big Sing*, first broadcast in 2001. "I think we were unique," says the former department head and *Songs of Praise* producer Michael Wakelin. "We were the only event to

Simply the best (2)

Equally at home with a millennium congregation of 70,000 and a chamber choir of five, conductor Paul Leddington Wright has probably seen it all on *Songs of Praise*. But even he was momentarily nonplussed at a choir rehearsal at Pershore Abbey in 1994 when the power supply cut out, plunging everything into impenetrable black. Commandeering from somewhere a tiny pencil torch to read the score, he rehearsed the choir in total darkness for two hours until the final note was sung and, in a minor replay of Genesis chapter one, the power came on again and there was light.

But it was at the Christmas *Big Sing* of 2005 at the Royal Albert Hall that the sheer professionalism of the *Songs of Praise* operation struck him most forcefully. A forty-strong orchestra of some of the best musicians in the country had been assembled to accompany the adored Italian tenor Andrea Bocelli as he sang "Silent Night". Because he was generally used to singing with a full symphony orchestra of almost twice the size, Bocelli's management thought it better for him to perform to his pre-recorded backing track, leaving Paul Leddington Wright slightly disappointed that his hugely talented musicians would be merely miming. However, a problem with the recorded track prompted a rethink, and Paul persuaded the great man to sing with the live orchestra after all. There was just one problem. They were missing the harp part. The orchestra manager raced backstage to get it and discovered, to her horror, that there were *two* harp parts. With a mere shrug of her elegant shoulders harpist Skaila Kanga said, "Don't worry. I'll play both." The performance was a wild success. At the memory Paul says simply, "It was the epitome of professionalism all round. Such a lovely moment."

Top: Conductor Paul Leddington Wright.

Right: Andrea Bocelli.

Far right: The Royal Albert Hall, the venue of choice for the Big Sing.

go into the Albert Hall and get everyone to sing. They have various choirs there and things such as the Festival of Remembrance, but you don't get proper congregational singing. We flooded the place with 5,000 people and everybody sang."

A huge success in itself, the *Big Sing* has had its own spin-offs, too. An event this major and this popular would not only, it was hoped, bring choral singing to a new and younger audience, but also attract big-name talent which, in turn, would make it more popular still. "And its bedrock," says Hugh Faupel, "was congregational singing. The biggest Christian karaoke in the world. Singing is good for the soul. There is nothing quite like it. And when you experience it for yourself it makes you feel good. *Songs of Praise* is a feel-good programme. It is life-affirming."

But, as always, choice of music could prove divisive. Those who favour *Hymns Ancient and Modern*

Aled Jones presents the 2009 *Big Sing* at the Royal Albert Hall.

over the compositions of the new generation of hymn-writers such as Keith and Kristyn Getty, Stuart Townend, and Graham Kendrick have every right to their preference. But *Songs of Praise* was, in effect, gently reminding them that what is now ancient was once modern, and that what is now traditional was once unfamiliar, even revolutionary. And ought not the new generation of Christians, raised on the praise-band mix of drums, keyboards, guitar, bass, and lead vocals, to have its musical preferences reflected on the show too? *Songs of Praise*, mindful not to upset the same audience two weeks running, had (and still has) a delicate balance to strike.

The *Songs of Praise* producers, in collaboration with their music advisers and gifted conductors such as Paul Leddington Wright, Noel Tredinnick, and Gordon Stewart, straddle both traditions, deciding where, when, and how often the traditional should give way to the modern. Unsurprisingly they will not please everyone all the time. Hugh Faupel remembers being collared by an angry woman at one *Songs of Praise* broadcast, who made it clear that this modern stuff was not to her taste. Nor, while she was on the subject, were modern versions of the Bible. "Why are you messing around with the King James version?" she wondered. "If it was good enough for St Paul it should be good enough for you." On the other hand, he also remembers an elderly woman telling him how much she liked the new tunes once she had got used to them. "I just want to say that you make my day," came her appreciative response.

But even he would not – could not – abandon tradition entirely.

"I find the Christian faith endlessly interesting and hugely powerful. If you have a good Christian story well told you have a good piece of entertainment."

Michael Wakelin, former head of religious broadcasting

Amy Nuttall performing at the
Big Sing at the Royal Albert Hall
in 2009.

2009 Viewers' Questionnaire

In the 2009 viewers' questionnaire, the question "What do you most dislike about *Songs of Praise*?" prompted the answer "modern hymns", but also "old hymns", illustrating the difficulty in catering for the taste of every *Songs of Praise* viewer.

"My concern was to keep at the heart of the programme two or three or three of four traditional hymns in one way or another," he recalls. "I wanted to ensure that the older audience, whom I deeply respected, would not be left adrift. Even if the packaging was a little different I wanted them to know they would get 'Abide with Me' or 'Praise My Soul the King of Heaven' somewhere in the mix."

After the success of the first *Big Sing*, the programme caught the choir bug and began to develop choir-based programmes that have had an enormous impact on secular television both within the BBC and outside it. This began when Michael invited the record producer Pete Waterman, then a highly visible judge on the popular talent show *Pop Idol*, to be one

of the judges of a schools choir competition that he and Hugh had in mind for 2004. Part of the rationale was to bring in a younger audience and to promote choral singing in a popular way. This was all the more necessary, they believed, given that formal school assemblies, where Christian hymns had once been sung as a matter of routine, were becoming rarer and rarer. "*Songs of Praise* can reflect and feature great music," says Hugh, "and it can also champion great music. Ours was an attempt to contact a younger audience and enthuse them."

Enthuse the audience they certainly did. Michael remembers to this day the huge cheer that went up in the audience when Pete Waterman was announced, transforming a programme that, in all likelihood, had a dry and dusty reputation with youngsters into something almost cool. All of a sudden record companies and the music promoters sat up and took notice of what is one of the few truly popular music shows on British television. They were eager to offer their big-name stars to the show. "We are essentially a music entertainment show celebrating the Christian experience," says executive producer Tommy Nagra. "When you consider that music shows do not traditionally rate well on television, it says something

Pete Waterman, a keen railway enthusiast, is filmed on the footplate of a steam locomotive in 2003.

Tabloid storm in a teacup

In 2007 some newspapers reported that the *Songs of Praise* programme broadcast from Lichfield Cathedral that Easter had been recorded at the same time as the Advent programme of 2006 from the same cathedral. In the interests of economy this is a common practice, and the programme has always been open and honest about it. In fact every year the papers run a "fancy that" story about how the Christmas tree comes down and the daffodils go in. Only when somebody complained did the story acquire a negative spin.

"It costs a fortune to light these buildings," the former head of department Michael Wakelin says. "Would it be a good use of the licence payers' money to strip it all down, come back six months later, and stick it all back in again? No, it wouldn't. In fact the congregation loved the idea of wearing their spring outfits with their thermals on underneath."

that we still pull in millions of viewers each and every week."

The *Big Sing* had developed a momentum all of its own, attracting eager audiences from all corners of the British Isles and even, as the 2010 behind-the-scenes compilation showed, from Dallas, Texas. Looking back, it is easy to see why. Take the input of the legendary musical director Ray Monk, for example, who was drafted in to give the *Big Sing* his own unique treatment. A hugely respected figure in the popular music business, Monk had only to make a telephone call to deliver top-name vocalists and instrumentalists who

could lend any production the slick professionalism of a light entertainment spectacular.

But for that very reason the programme was moving into controversial territory. It was all very well investing in big

showcase editions involving the likes of Bryn Terfel, Katherine Jenkins, and Russell Watson, and it was all very well giving them the popular light entertainment feel, but was this straying too far from the programme's brief?

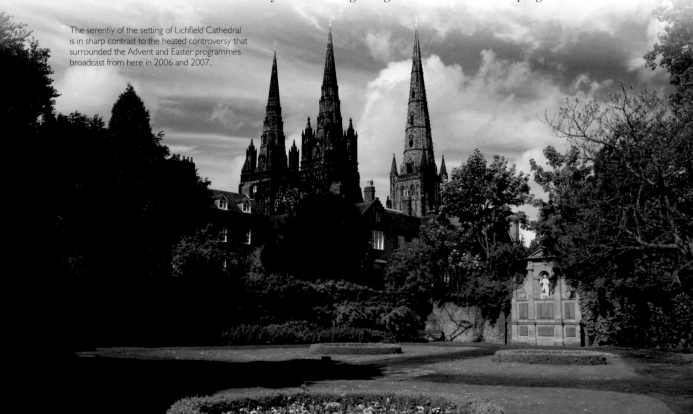

The serenity of the setting of Lichfield Cathedral is in sharp contrast to the heated controversy that surrounded the Advent and Easter programmes broadcast from here in 2006 and 2007.

Michael Wakelin admits that they sometimes got it wrong but, on balance, defends the radical shift the programme made. "When we got it right we got some big names and eye-catching programmes. Society was changing, the church was changing. We were right to add a bit more colour, flair, and celebrity to *Songs of Praise.*"

Besides, the *Big Sing* was not broadcast every week, and Michael could point to more conventional editions that had celebrated Easter in Bury St Edmund's, Pentecost in Exeter, or Christmas in Ely. But both he and Hugh felt that the programme had to move on and, in an era when organ-based singing is not the only musical form of the Christian experience, that it has

to reflect the diversity of musical styles throughout the country.

What *Songs of Praise* does to this day is to use a venue to the maximum, filming extra material to use in subsequent programmes. So, when visiting a cathedral, for example, the team will spend maybe three or four days there recording two standard programmes and collecting material for a third and fourth. Lighting and sound engineers (legends such as Bernie Davis and Geoff Stafford, who won a Royal Television Society craft award for their lighting effects) will work creative miracles transforming the nave into a mini recording studio, where local choral societies may be invited to perform. The footage will later form the basis of

a choir-led programme rather than one which is congregation-centred.

It might also feature in one of the many themed programmes that *Songs of Praise* broadcasts from time to time to introduce variety into the mix. The producers choose themes such as forgiveness, love, justice, light, or hope, and weave around these abstractions material that is rooted in the everyday realities of people's lives. Or they may choose tangible objects such as gardens, stained glass, gifts, or flowers as a starting point for a spiritual reflection celebrated in story and song. The ever-adaptable *Songs of Praise* team takes advantage of the chosen location to film people and places that can fit into programmes other than the one they have primarily come to make. Perhaps with Jesus' feeding of the 5,000 in mind, they set to the task of producing more from less and, with no drop in quality, have continued

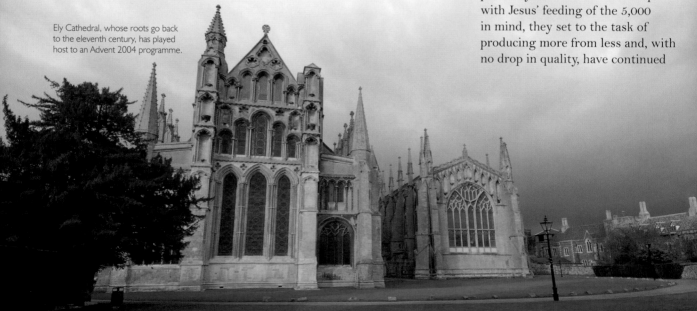

Ely Cathedral, whose roots go back to the eleventh century, has played host to an Advent 2004 programme.

On the trail of the Wesleys

In 2007 *Songs of Praise* featured two programmes to mark the 300th anniversary of the birth of the prolific hymn-writer Charles Wesley. The singing was recorded at Wesley's Chapel in London and the location filming took place around the United Kingdom, including in Bristol (where he lived) and London (where he died).

Remarkably, in 1735, Charles sailed with his brother John to Georgia in the United States of America, as a missionary to the new colony. He served as the secretary of the governor, General James Oglethorpe, but became ill in the extremely hot conditions and had to return home earlier than planned. To reflect this aspect of Wesley's story, *Songs of Praise* flew to Georgia to film several exclusive interviews with leading Methodists and to reconstruct dramatic scenes from the past.

The producer at the time, David Taviner, recalls the searing temperatures and the challenge of the shoot: "Though the film crew were sweating buckets, I can only imagine how the actors felt who were dressed in period costume. Local volunteers were enormously patient as we re-created moments in time from the eighteenth century. But travelling to this part of America was also a wonderful reminder of how this short period in Wesley's life influenced his Christian conversion and his life-long passion for prose that has resulted in a legacy of at least 5,000 hymns, many of which remain so inspirational 300 years later."

"I think the Royal Albert Hall lends itself perfectly to the Big Sing. It's circular, so we all feel as one voice singing in honour and praise to God."

Ken Burton, music director of the Adventist Vocal Ensemble

to produce modern-day television miracles of their own.

Alongside the themed programmes, *Songs of Praise* also considers it vital to mark key dates in the Christian calendar. These include Christmas, Easter, and Pentecost, of course, but also the great historical events that saw the faith fashioned into the shape it is today. One such programme marked the abolition of the slave trade in the British Empire and was broadcast on 25 March 2007 – 200 years to the day after the legislation was passed in parliament. It followed a group of Christians travelling to Gambia to take part in a symbolic act of atonement for the sins of their forebears, and was memorable

for the extraordinarily moving encounter between Vonetta Winter, descendant of a slave family, and Andrew Hawkins, descendant of the sixteenth-century captain and slave trader Sir John Hawkins. After a public ceremony attended by the vice-president of Gambia, the programme filmed a very personal and intimate moment when Vonetta and Andrew embraced in a tearful acknowledgment, not only of the wrongs done in the past, but also of the reconciliation that, after repentance and forgiveness, is possible in the present.

The African-American spirituals that featured in this programme were sung by the bass baritone Sir Willard White made for original and powerful television, and they contribute to the richness and variety that *Songs of Praise* needs if it is to develop and grow. But loyal fans need not fear that the programme has turned its back on its original vision. "This is a flagship Christian programme," says the current executive producer, Tommy Nagra. "Congregational hymn-singing will

continue to be at the very heart of the show. That's what our core audience want and they tell us so week by week." If there is one man who understands more than most the power of that hymn-singing tradition, it is the composer and national ambassador for singing, Howard Goodall, who in 2010 also served as a judge on the *Songs of Praise* schools choir competition. A self-confessed "anorak" when it comes to hymns, he admits that as a

"I'm a Methodist chapel boy and the church taught us from a very early age that [singing] brings communities together through friendship, through religion."

Bryn Terfel, bass baritone

boy he collected hymn-books in the way most boys collected stamps. "Hymns belong to all of us," he says, "and *Songs of Praise* above all is a celebration of the best in hymn-singing. There's something wonderful about the sense of permanence of *Songs of Praise* in our life on a Sunday evening. Of course it will inevitably change and develop as society changes, but what it constantly does is involve you in a world you don't much see elsewhere on television."

Tommy Nagra knows well that he is heir to and guardian of a unique broadcasting institution that strives to maintain its popularity by ensuring that the channels of communication with its audience remain constantly open. "When the audience tells us what it wants, we listen," says Tommy. "We are forever looking at ways of measuring audience appreciation and I would worry if appreciation for the programme showed even the slightest signs of dipping. But it hasn't yet and we as a team are committed to ensuring it doesn't."

Composer Howard Goodall.

Every letter that comes into the Manchester HQ receives a reply from a member of the team, and any suggestion that is made is carefully considered. "We listen to our audience," says Tommy. "They dictate the show. We rely on them because they are the content of the programme. If they don't turn up in fine voice, we don't *have* a programme." Shortly after

Tommy took the helm in 2009, and reviewed the team to meet the challenges of the new decade, the programme commissioned a snap survey gauging audience reaction to the show. A questionnaire was distributed at the *Big Sing* asking why, and how frequently, people watched the programme and what they most and least enjoyed about it. The questionnaire generally

Pam Rhodes

Favourite hymns: "Let There Be Peace on Earth", "Eternal Father Strong to Save".

"I love *Songs of Praise* because it's so much more than just television. Time and again we hear how it touches people's lives. Our interviewees speak of human experience from the heart. They describe what they've been through and what they've learned, and their honesty reaches out to ring chords of recognition in viewers who might well be struggling with similar feelings. My job is to draw out the facts people need to know, as well as those heart-stopping insights into the struggle, fear, sadness, triumph, and inspirational faith which underpin so many of the stories we feature. Recording those intimate, moving interviews takes time, care, and trust; and over the years I've had the privilege of sharing heart-warming conversations with many wonderful people of courage and commitment. It's not surprising that viewers are as inspired by those interviewees as I am. They may switch on to sing along with the hymns – but it's those people who speak so generously between the music who really touch hearts and memories.

Being a *Songs of Praise* presenter is not just a job – it's a responsibility, lovingly undertaken. And twenty-three years on, I still love every minute of it."

"On lots of TV programmes people are there to be laughed at. On Songs of Praise they are cared for."

Garry Boon, producer

invited them to sum up their thoughts about a programme they clearly loved. The results were instructive and, along with other research and spontaneous audience feedback, have informed the thinking behind the current team's efforts.

The overwhelming viewer reaction was that the programme is in good heart and fine voice. "The spiritual backbone of Great Britain," wrote one. "A programme that lifts you up when you are feeling low," wrote another. Others expressed their approval with observations such as, "It's inspiring, uplifting and full of sheer joy", "It's part of our heritage and culture", "It's a source of happiness to my soul", and "One of the best programmes the BBC has ever done." Of course some preferred the traditional hymns, while others asked for more modern ones to be included, but all looked forward to people's stories ("the testimonies of ordinary people's faith experiences", as one viewer put it). Interestingly, although the programme is not designed as an act of worship, a fair few praised it for bringing a sense of reverence into the home: "A life-line for those who can't attend church services"; "It's like going to church without leaving the house." Or, with due apology to the clergy, "All the nice parts of going to church – without going." All of which confirms Tommy Nagra's view that a number of different audiences are tuning in, either regularly or from time to time. One, naturally, is the committed, loyal core of viewers who are the bedrock of the *Songs of Praise* phenomenon ("our season-ticket holders", as Tommy puts it). The other is that group of people who, for one reason or another, cannot get to church on Sunday evening but who still feel the need for the experience of devotional music that has been at the heart of *Songs of Praise* for fifty successful years. The third audience includes those "of vague faith" who may not belong to any formal religious denomination (and who certainly do not define themselves in terms of church attendance) but who still feel an inexplicable pull toward the sort of spiritual experience that the programme strives to provide. But perhaps Tommy would be most gratified by one viewer who, when asked why he watched the programme, wrote simply, "It's a family tradition." And the most common complaint about the programme? That it is not long enough.

Two programmes, broadcast in successive weeks in 2010, illustrate *Songs of Praise*'s distinctive mix of the old and the new. And yet both could equally lay claim to being "traditional" and could say with equal justification that they were part of the unbroken line stretching between 1961 and today. Pam Rhodes's visit to Winchester was perhaps more obviously exemplary, with its historical survey of the cathedral and its

A 2010 programme saw Pam Rhodes visit England's oldest almshouses at the Hospital of St Cross, Winchester, where she talked to some of the Brothers who live there.

contemporary exploration of the lives of the people living in the nearby almshouses. In focusing on both people and places it shone its unique light on a corner of English life and characteristically enriched the entire experience with singing broadcast from one of the most distinctive and venerable Christian sites in the country.

The following week Aled turned up (on the pillion of a chauffeur's motorcycle) at the doors of the Royal Albert Hall ready to present a behind-the-scenes look at preparations for the 2010 *Big Sing*, incorporating unseen footage from the previous year's stunningly successful event. This is not the hyperbole of an enthusiast, but a fair reflection of the audience reaction on the night. "It's just a wonderful way to glorify God. You just feel so uplifted by it,"

said one member of the audience. Another, a Salvation Army captain (and therefore no stranger to fine music), said, "When you stand among 5,000 people and they're all singing the same hymns, it gives you such inspiration. It gives you something to face tomorrow."

And what a show it was! Cameras swooped and hovered, pulled back and zoomed in, capturing both the totality of the event and the intimacy of each singer praising God. Every seat, every tier, every row, every box was filled with people singing their hearts out. Camera operators – heirs to the great tradition that Ray Short had pioneered nearly fifty years before – framed singers in twos and threes and fours, sometimes singly,

R 1   VTR 2   VTR 3   VTR 5   VTR 6

Llew   VTR 1

PVW   TX

Brian   2 Grant   3 Russ

Sitting in front of an array of monitors in the scanner, the director is able to view each of the shots being offered from individual cameras at the same time.

the Royal Albert Hall, ensuring that the expensive broadcasting equipment brought in for the Proms could be reused for *Songs of Praise* without being taken down. This, too, was a direct link with the thinking fifty years ago, when executives realised that the OB facilities used for Saturday sport could be pressed into service for Sunday worship. Not only that, *two* programmes were recorded on the same day, allowing the event to be enjoyed twice – once in the autumn and once at Christmas. And however appalled the tabloid press might claim to have been by the Lichfield quick-change act, the audience did not falter when unseasonal Christmas trees were unselfconsciously trundled in to re-dress the set for a second show. On the contrary, people were filmed

sometimes in groups, creating a living tableau that was much more (and much less) than a performance. The *Songs of Praise* series editor, David Taviner, put his finger on it when he said, "There's a real sense of worship. It's not just a sing-along. And everybody who watches it at home on TV will feel that they're here in the Royal Albert Hall themselves." The soul diva Ruby Turner, steeped in the gospel tradition, echoed David when she stressed the community focus of the whole event, saying simply, "It's very important that the audience feels like they are part of it."

Aled's programme also demonstrated the work of the BBC's technical crews at their most efficient best. Electricians, carpenters, sound engineers, and lighting riggers were all expertly choreographed by production

supervisors who knew how to make the most of their resources and their staff, and to use the licence payers' money (your money) economically. Preparations for the *Big Sing*, for example, took place as soon as the *Last Night of the Proms* had been broadcast from

Soul diva Ruby Turner, a guest on the 2009 *Big Sing*.

"You can't work on this programme for long without being touched by people's lives."

Pam Rhodes, presenter

eating their sandwiches and ice creams between takes, thoroughly enjoying the rare treat of seeing how the magic *really* comes together.

In the audience that day, filling in the anonymous questionnaire that the team was distributing, was one woman who had an intriguing observation to make. She was happy with the programme generally but felt the need to point out what she believed was an omission. "You never interview anyone," she wrote, "who says adversity has felt like God giving them a kick in the teeth. It happens." The team took this clearly heartfelt observation seriously, and recognised something analogous to "compassion fatigue" – the impression that we have heard so many stories of triumph over adversity that their real power has been diluted or lost altogether. Or, indeed, that such stories have a hollow ring when set against experiences of suffering that do

not always have happy endings. Researchers and producers have to sift through the stories they unearth and make a careful and sensitive choice, varying both the tone and the content of what will be heard in any one programme.

And yet had this unknown respondent watched the programme on the theme of prayer which was broadcast in March 2010 (and, given that her questionnaire also mentioned the valuable part that *Songs of Praise* played in her own prayer life, she probably *did* watch it) she would have seen her reservations dealt with in the most sensitive and quite astonishing way. She and some 3 million viewers will have seen Aled's interview with the remarkable Jane Grayshon, who had been in constant pain following complications after an appendix operation thirty-four years before. There were no easy answers to Aled's questions. Life, she said, *was* hard – "Hell on earth sometimes." Yes, she felt very angry that the Almighty had seen fit to allow such suffering to befall her and she often prayed that it would go away. And yes, she often wished that she were not here "because heaven will be so much better than here. No more pain."

But over time she learned to accept that "being me is being in pain" and, with an understated altruism that scarcely did justice

One of Pam Rhodes's most memorable experiences presenting *Songs of Praise* was when she met Pope John Paul II, March 1997.

to her extraordinary strength and courage, she explained how she "had to learn not to long for death in a way that would hurt other people". It is a hard heart that is not moved by this. And, hearing it, surely no one could accuse *Songs of Praise* of avoiding the realities of life, of sugar-coating the Christian experience, or of sanitising the lives of ordinary people for the sake of a feel-good sing-along. No, these are the lived lives of people we may meet on the bus or pass in the street, people we may not know personally but whose experiences, happy or sombre, mirror our own. The quiet struggles, private sacrifices, and hidden inner strengths of such people are celebrated in words and memorialised in song every week so that we can all gain a better understanding of what it means to be truly alive. There are no guaranteed happy endings but, as in the final shot from flood-ravaged Cockermouth, where we began, there will always be a rainbow.

Since the first *Songs of Praise* aired in 1961, the television landscape has changed irrevocably. Then there were only two channels, broadcasting in black and white to a population largely in awe of the new technology. Contrast that with the hundreds of terrestrial and satellite stations from all over the world beaming high-definition programmes into the homes of today's sophisticated and demanding audiences, twenty-four hours a day. With competition like this, there are few programmes that can regularly guarantee audiences in the millions, and none that have done so for as long as *Songs of Praise*.

But the programme has never been complacent. It knows that to stand still is to be overtaken and that it must move with the times if it is to be contemporary and relevant to people's lives. However, *Songs of Praise* proceeds by evolution not revolution and no one need fear that the programme they have loved for decades is about to change overnight. What it will do, however, is take full advantage of all the emerging technologies – just as it has been doing for fifty glorious years – to make the programmes that viewers want. And, if anything, there will be more of the *Songs of Praise* experience to enjoy: more interviews available to download as podcasts; more behind-the-scenes footage to access when the main programme has been viewed; more buttons to press to vary how, where, and when the "nation's favourite" is watched; more hymns to enjoy via the internet or the iPlayer, or contraptions still to be invented. And all of this, of course, is in addition to the regular programme that has been lovingly prepared, week by week, for fifty years, to be

delivered, gift-wrapped, into your homes every Sunday evening.

These are exciting times for the programme as it prepares to meet the challenges of tomorrow while staying true to the vision it embraced all those years ago. The fiftieth is, by any standards, a remarkable anniversary. The talented men and women who have kept *Songs of Praise* on the road for so long will rightly look back on the past with pride. But it is the millions of people in towns and villages across the nation that hold the programme's future in their hands. It is they, after all, who open their hearts to strangers every week, trusting that the spiritual impulses that sustain them may, just for a moment, come to life in song and thereby enhance all our lives. And it is, has been, and always will be on them – on you – that *Songs of Praise* depends.

Picture Acknowledgments

Every effort has been made to trace copyright holders and to obtain their permission for the use of copyright material. The publisher apologises for any errors or omissions in the list below and would be grateful to be notified of any corrections that should be incorporated in future reprints or editions of this book.

Alamy: p. 11 ClassicStock; p. 12–13 PhotoStock-Israel; p. 32b Imagestate Media Partners Limited - Impact Photos; pp. 35, 95 Pictorial Press Ltd; p. 67 Justin Kase z09z; p. 90t Andrea Jones; p. 92–93 Jeremy Inglis

Andrew Barr: pp. 10, 16, 34br, 41–42, 44, 52–53, 55, 65–66, 68, 70t

BBC: pp. 6, 14–15, 18t, 22t, 23, 24–25, 26br, 28tr, 28br, 31, 32t, 33b, 34t, 37, 46, 48tl, 49–51, 57b, 58br, 59bl, 61b, 62–63, 72tr, 82, 83t, 84–85t, 86, 89, 91, 93c, 93b, 94, 96tl, 96bc, 97, 98–99, 102, 104–105, 108

Bob Prizeman: pp. 27, 78–79

Cathy Osfarnie: p. 20t

Chris Darwin p. 21r

Chris Goor: p. 73

Chris Mann: pp. 19, 24t, 25tl, 30, 38, 54, 58tl, 59tr, 60, 61tl, 61tr, 69, 70b, 74–75, 81

Corbis: pp. 17, 48–49 Adam Woolfitt; pp. 18, 107 Tim Graham; p. 24c Pascal Saez; p. 45 Hulton-Deutsch Collection; p. 56 BBC; p. 76 Atlantide Phototravel; p. 80 Destinations; p. 88 Ocean; p. 96br Roberto Herrett/Loop Images; p. 101 David Pillinger

David Taviner: p. 64

DIPR/Tony Cunnane: p. 12

Francesca Williams: p. 8

Geoff Stafford: p. 26t

Getty: pp. 33, 87; p. 22 AFP; p. 90b Tim Graham

iStock: p. 39 Eneri LLC

James Tinsley: p. 43

John Forrest: p. 83, 84bl

Judith Sharp: p. 52

Lisa Ashton: pp. 20b, 103

Liverpool Daily Post and Echo: p. 85

Lucy Wilson: p. 100

Pam Rhodes: pp. 21t, 81t, 93t, 109

Peter Greenyer: p. 77

Radio Times Magazine: pp. 28, 40, 47

Richard Carruthers: pp. 57t, 72tl

Sally Magnusson: p. 36

Sian Salt: p. 25br

Source unknown: p. 21r

Tom Ritchie: p. 26bl

Valetta Stallabrass: p. 20c